THE HARMLESS NECESSARY CAT

A World War II Family Saga in Allied-Occupied Iran

Sepehr Haddad

APPLEYARD & SONS PUBLISHING

OTHER WORKS BY
SEPEHR HADDAD:

A HUNDRED SWEET PROMISES

Winner of the 2023 American Fiction Awards
Historical Fiction & Historical Romance

Disclaimer

This book is inspired by a true story but remains a work of fiction. While many characters and events are based on real people and occurrences, they have been fictionalized for the narrative. Other characters, incidents, and dialogues, except for certain well-known historical figures, are entirely the products of the author's imagination and should not be regarded as factual. When historical figures are featured, the events, incidents, and dialogues involving them are fictionalized and not intended to reflect actual occurrences.

Copyright © 2024 Sepehr Haddad

All rights reserved. No part of this book may be reproduced in any form or by any electronic or mechanical means, including information storage and retrieval systems, without permission in writing from the publisher, except by a reviewer who may quote brief passages in a review.

Cover Concept: Sepehr Haddad
Cover Design: Ebooklaunch.com
APPLEYARD & SONS PUBLISHING
5557 Baltimore Ave., Suite 500-1108
Hyattsville, Maryland, 20781
AppleyardandSonsPublishing.com

Print ISBN 978-1-7325943-3-3
Ebook ISBN 978-1-7325943-4-0
Library of Congress Control Number: 2024914736

Dedication

In loving memory of my father, Jamal,
who inspired me with his stories.

Acknowledgments

Thank you, Moana, my fellow traveler,
through every page of this novel's journey.

CONTENTS

Author's Note i
Part I: The Pre-War Years 1
   Chapter 1 3
   Chapter 2 7
   Chapter 3 15
   Chapter 4 23
   Chapter 5 28
   Chapter 6 35
   Chapter 7 40
   Chapter 8 50
   Chapter 9 60
Part II: The War Years 65
   Chapter 10 67
   Chapter 11 75
   Chapter 12 91
   Chapter 13 97
   Chapter 14 107
   Chapter 15 119
   Chapter 16 127
   Chapter 17 134
   Chapter 18 144
   Chapter 19 149
   Chapter 20 162
   Chapter 21 168
   Chapter 22 174
   Chapter 23 185

Chapter 24 189
Chapter 25 200
Chapter 26 207
Chapter 27 218
Chapter 28 225
Chapter 29 233
Chapter 30 242
Chapter 31 247
Part III: The Post-War Years 261
Chapter 32 263
Chapter 33 269
Chapter 34 273
Epilogue 291

"…The line separating good and evil passes not through states, nor between classes, nor between political parties either— but right through every human heart.

This line shifts. Inside us, it oscillates with the years.

And even within hearts overwhelmed by evil, one small bridgehead of good is retained. And even in the best of all hearts, there remains…an unuprooted small corner of evil."

Aleksander Solzhenitsyn

Author's Note

Because this novel is set in Iran, I want to provide a historical background of the country once known as Persia. Persia often conjures images of an exotic and ancient civilization rich in history and culture; however, since the Islamic Revolution of 1979, Iran has been viewed through a different lens. Understanding the country's complex and multifaceted history is crucial to appreciating this story.

Nestled in the Middle East, Iran stands at the crossroads of three vast continents: Asia, Africa, and Europe. In the late 19th and early 20th centuries, foreign powers cast their gaze upon Iran, drawn by its strategic position wedged between British-occupied India, Imperial Russia, and the Ottoman Empire. But it was not only geography that beckoned these outsiders. Iran's abundant oil reserves played an increasingly influential role in their calculations.

In 1901, a British magnate named William Knox D'Arcy struck a momentous deal with an Iranian Shah of the Qajar dynasty, securing an astonishing 60-year oil concession and acquiring a treasure that would shape the world's destiny.

In exchange, the Iranians received a paltry sum of 20,000 British pounds, some shares in D'Arcy's enterprise, and a meager 16 percent of the future profits. In 1909, the Anglo-Iranian Oil Company (APOC) was born from D'Arcy's ambition. In 1914, the British government stepped in, purchasing a controlling 51 percent of the shares, effectively nationalizing the oil company. APOC would eventually transform into what is now known as British Petroleum (BP).

But the scramble for Iran's riches did not end with D'Arcy's triumphant coup. In the Anglo-Russian Treaty of 1907, the Russian and British governments conspired to carve Persia into two distinct spheres of influence.

The Russians claimed the northern expanse adjacent to their recently conquered dominions in Transcaucasia. Meanwhile, the British chose the country's southern parts, skirting their imperial prize of India.

Thus, a third region emerged — a buffer zone — intended to keep the disputes of these European powers at bay. This treaty marked the culmination of decades of engaging in the captivating game of wits between Russian and British interests, a high-stakes theater that became known as the "Great Game."

Iran, steadfast in its declaration of neutrality during both World Wars, found itself swept up in the tempest of European powers' disregard for such proclamations. In the wake of these tumultuous times, the country became an unwilling stage for foreign occupation.

During World War I, Iran endured a grueling trial of economic hardship exacerbated by a severe drought. The unforgiving combination birthed a scourge of famine and disease, exacting a terrible toll on the Iranian people. Starvation claimed the lives of more than a million souls, victims of malnutrition and the afflictions it wrought — cholera, typhus, and deadly influenza that swept across the globe in the waning days of the war.

World War II brought a chilling sense of déjà vu to Iran's doorsteps as British and Soviet troops descended upon the land in 1941.

Despite the volumes devoted to World War II, little is known of Iran's trials during that global conflict. Many remember the Japanese surprise assault on Pearl Harbor in 1941, epitomizing deceitful warfare, just as Operation Barbarossa, Hitler's treacherous invasion of the Soviet Union in the same year, played a parallel tune of unexpected aggression. Yet, there was another lesser-known clandestine maneuver, one that history often overlooks. While these significant activities gripped the world's attention, the Allies, driven by strategic interests, launched a sneak attack on neutral Iran.

In the grand tapestry of the war, it might seem a minor thread. Still, its implications were intricately woven into the fabric of the more significant conflict. Orchestrated primarily by British and Soviet forces, this covert operation was driven by concerns over Iran's neutral stance and questionable affiliations with Germany as the Allies coveted the nation's oil riches.

The advancing tide of Hitler's forces in Russia fanned the flames of their fears as they perceived a threat to their precious oil supply lines. The Allies seized control of the Trans-Iranian Railroad and trucks owned by the public and private sectors. A cruel twist of fate, for this, occurred precisely as the 1941 harvest unfolded its promise.

The Soviets, claiming the northern reaches of Iran, halted the flow of food shipments to the Iranian populace, citing their dire need to sustain Russian troops engaged in fierce battles against the German war machine.

And thus, history, as it so often does, repeated itself. The ramifications were significant, for they disrupted the core of the nation's sustenance, affecting 75 percent of Iran's food distribution system. Famine and disease descended upon the land. With its relentless grip, starvation this time claimed the lives of millions more Iranians – ushering in a sorrowful chapter of suffering and despair.

While researching and writing this novel, I was in awe of the Iranian spirit – a testament to a civilization's resilience. Despite invasions, conquests, and shifting sands of time, the Iranian heart has endured, proving that authentic culture and identity are not just rooted in the land but in the collective memory of its people.

From the tales of Ferdowsi's Shahnameh to the verses of Rumi and Hafez, Iran's ethos thrives undiminished and unbroken. Every note of the setar, every motif on a Persian carpet, speaks of a history that refuses to be forgotten.

This spirit has withstood the test of time, not because it resists change but because it absorbs, evolves, and remains profoundly Iranian. In the face of war, occupation, and socio-political transformations, the core of Iranian identity has found a way to live on, anchored in rich traditions that predate even the oldest invasions.

TIMELINE OF IRANIAN HISTORY (1907-1946)

1907 - Anglo-Russian Agreement

Iran was divided into Russian and British spheres of influence, with Russia controlling the north and Britain controlling the south, reducing Iran to a semi-colonial state.

1914-1918 - World War I

Iran became a battlefield for Russian, Turkish, and British troops despite declaring neutrality.

1921 - Coup d'état by Reza Khan

The beginning of the Pahlavi dynasty's rise to power.

1925 — Establishment of the Pahlavi Dynasty

Reza Shah Pahlavi's coronation, significant modernization efforts were initiated.

1939 — World War II

Iran declared neutrality.

1941 — Anglo-Soviet Invasion of Iran and Abdication of Reza Shah

Russia & Britain invaded Iran and forced Reza Shah's abdication; his son, Mohammad Reza Pahlavi, became Shah.

1943 — Iran Declares War on Germany; The Tehran Conference

Iran sided with the Allies against the Axis powers; Churchill, Roosevelt, and Stalin met in Tehran.

1945 — End of World War II

Withdrawal of British and American troops; Soviet troops remained.

1946 — Soviet Withdrawal from Iran

End of Soviet occupation, a diplomatic victory for Iran.

A World War II Family Saga in Allied-Occupied Iran

Part I: The Pre-War Years

Chapter 1

"Tradition is a guide and not a jailer."
W. Somerset Maugham

Qazvin, 1925

Massoumeh finally convinced herself to do it. Old traditions have a way of imprisoning a young mind, but she believed this was her only escape. With a sob in her throat, she closed her eyes and stepped onto the icy railing. Her legs trembled as she stood precariously on the edge, trying not to peek down.

A frigid wind clawed at her face, mirroring the chill curdling in her gut. A blanket of freshly fallen snow lay beneath the balcony, its tranquility masking the storm brewing inside her. Meanwhile, Fatima, her devoted servant girl, prepared for her evening prayers in a nearby room.

The world tilted, vertigo twisting Massoumeh's stomach, but it was nothing compared to the churning despair consuming her. A final prayer escaped her lips, not to God, but to the oblivion waiting.

Gathering all the courage she could, she leaped.

The wind buffeted Massoumeh, the cold stealing her breath. The ground rushed up to meet her, a monstrous maw ready to devour. But then, a shock. Not the bone-shattering impact she expected, but a soft, yielding embrace. A towering mound of snow, a remnant of an earlier storm piled high by the diligent gardener, became an unlikely savior.

Hearing the thud, Fatima initially thought a tree branch had fallen from the weight of the recent snowfall. She rushed out of her room and found Massoumeh semi-conscious. Fatima screamed for help, oblivious to Massoumeh's attempt to abort the child she had been carrying for the past seven months.

Fatima gasped. The fall and the impact sent the unborn child into turmoil. When the other servants arrived, Fatima ordered them to hurry and fetch the midwife; it looked like Massoumeh was about to deliver the baby.

Massoumeh regained consciousness, clutching her stomach tightly, telling Fatima, whose worried face was illuminated by the oil lamp she held aloft, that she was in great pain.

When the pain subsided, Fatima asked, "*Khanoom*, (Ma'am), what happened? How did you fall from the balcony?"

"I didn't fall," Massoumeh choked out, her voice low. "I jumped."

"Why did you jump, especially when you are expecting?" Fatima inquired.

Massoumeh, her pain returning and fading again, responded with labored breath, "I didn't want this baby; I wanted to end it. I overheard the other servants murmuring that I am now only a *dokhtarza* (a woman who only gives birth to girls)."

"But Khanoom, you have already given birth to your son Arash; what they say is ridiculous," Fatima replied.

Massoumeh began to pass in and out of consciousness. "Yes, …but the next two were girls…, and I'm sure this one is, too."

The Harmless Necessary Cat

The midwife arrived and delivered Massoumeh's baby two months earlier than expected. That night, the whispers of dokhtarza echoing in her ear would be silenced. The family would wait until Massoumeh's husband, Mohammad, returned from his business trip to Baku in Russia so he could name the boy.

After the birth, the household buzzed with activity. The servants who once gossiped behind closed doors now marveled at the health of the premature infant. Despite his early arrival, the baby was strong, and his cries resonated through the halls, declaring his fragile yet fierce will to live.

Massoumeh, weak but relieved, lay in bed with her newborn swaddled beside her. She watched him with exhaustion and wonder as if seeing a glimmer of hope she did not anticipate. Fatima stood by her side, her loyalty unshaken, brimming with questions.

"Fatima," Massoumeh breathed, her voice urgent, "you must promise me something."

Fatima nodded slowly, concern etched on her face. "Anything, Khanoom," she replied, her voice steady despite the night's chaos.

"Promise me you will tell the others I slipped. Let them believe it was an accident. They must never know I tried to end my baby's life."

Massoumeh's voice broke, "I feel such tremendous guilt, Fatima. I almost took his life before he had a chance to live. Promise me."

Fatima's eyes glistened. Her lips formed a silent affirmation, a solemn vow. "I promise, Khanoom, with my life. I will tell no one."

Then, focusing on the child, she added with conviction, "And he will never know, as God is my witness."

As dawn broke over Qazvin, the first rays of sunlight pierced through the curtains, casting a warm glow on the mother and child. Massoumeh drifted into a fitful sleep. Her dreams were haunted by the weight of her actions, the overwhelming guilt of what she had almost done, and the fragile life she now held in her arms.

Massoumeh's husband, Mohammad, returned from his trip to Baku a few days later. Upon seeing his newborn son for the first time, he named me Sohrab.

CHAPTER 2

"What's in a name? that which we call a rose
By any other name would smell as sweet."

William Shakespeare

My father was a businessman, an importer of iron products from Russia, who, in return, exported cotton to them. Back then, identity was shaped by one's lineage or livelihood. Individuals were recognized as "Sohrab, son of Mohammad," or by their trade, "Mohammad, the iron merchant," and occasionally, their place of origin, with surnames like "Tehrani," denoting a heritage rooted in Tehran.

The government mandate to adopt surnames saw my father embracing *Ahangar*—the Persian word for a worker in iron or a blacksmith, a nod to his profession as an importer of iron goods.

A fervent patriot, he sought a family name rooted in Persian culture. Inspired by Kaveh Ahangar, the legendary figure who vanquished tyranny in the poet Ferdowsi's epic *Shahnameh* (The Book of Kings), my father chose names for his offspring from this revered text.

My older brother was named Arash, in homage to the saga's valiant Arash the Archer *(Arash-e Kamangir)*. I was named Sohrab, after the son of the folk hero Rostam and his lover, Princess Tahmineh.

Growing up, my father often shared tales from the Shahnameh. Among these stories, of course, the name that resonated with me was Sohrab. It was not just a name; it was a legacy my father cherished and bestowed upon me, hoping that I, too, would embody the virtues of loyalty and honor that defined the legendary hero.

As my namesake's story is told by Ferdowsi, Rostam, a great Iranian warrior, is searching for his missing horse, *Rakhsh*. Rostam selected Rakhsh for his remarkable strength and enduring stamina, a horse matched by no other. Such was their bond that Rakhsh would accept no rider but Rostam, acknowledging only the warrior as his true master. Indeed, Rakhsh was the sole steed capable of bearing Rostam's formidable weight and power—any other mount would succumb beneath him.

Described as possessing the broad chest and shoulders of a lion, coupled with the mighty strength of an elephant, Rakhsh stood as a stallion of unrivaled courage and loyalty. His striking coat shimmered like rose petals strewn across a saffron canvas, a wondrous and awe-inspiring sight.

Rostam ventures into a foreign land in his quest to find Rakhsh. During his stay, he is hosted by the king of the realm. One night, the king's daughter, Princess Tahmina, who is well aware of Rostam's valor, stealthily visits his chamber. Captivated by his fame, she declares her love for him and proposes a bargain: she will ensure Rakhsh's return if he agrees to father her child.

Rostam and his horse Rakhsh - Mashhad, Iran.

They spend the night in a loving embrace, Tahmina is impregnated, and Rostam's horse is returned the following day. Before his departure, Rostam entrusts Tahmina with two symbols of their fleeting union.

For a daughter, a jewel to be placed in her hair, a gleam amidst locks, signifying the light of their union. For a son, a seal, to be fastened around his arm, a tribute to his heritage and strength.

Time marched forward, and a son was born from their union, whom Tahmina named Sohrab. As the years passed, father and son's paths remained diverged until a war between the two neighboring countries led to a tumultuous crescendo, and the two men found themselves ensnared by fate clashing on the battlefield.

Neither man knows their opponent's name, though Sohrab is familiar with his father's reputation but is unaware that he is fighting him. The subsequent battle is a whirlwind of emotion and brute strength, culminating in Rostam's heartrending victory over his flesh and blood.

With his dying breath, Sohrab envisions an act of retribution that would never come. Showing Rostam the same amulet he gave Tahmina the night of their union, Sohrab declares that his father would take revenge. Ironically, the princess gave the amulet to Sohrab to keep him safe in the war. Sohrab dies, forever a stranger to the truth—that his father was the very instrument of his demise.

🐱🐱🐱

As a child, I reveled in the grandeur of these stories. Sohrab was a figure of immense strength and unyielding integrity, a beacon of courage and nobility. His deeds took root in my imagination, filling me with a comforting sense of connection to a lineage of Iranian heroes as if I carried a piece of that ancient valor within me.

As I grew older, the weight of my name became more palpable. I was keenly aware of the chasm between the heroism of my namesake and my unremarkable existence. Sohrab, the stalwart warrior, stood in sharp contrast to the ordinary boy who bore his name. The juxtaposition was humbling, an ever-present reminder of the greatness I was supposedly tied to, but a greatness that seemed utterly beyond my reach.

I was no hero—far from it. Often timid and afraid, my life lacked the noble quests that defined Sohrab's story. My challenges were mundane, my victories small and personal.

Despite this, there was a quiet strength in knowing my name's origin. The tales of the Shahnameh, with their grand mosaic of gallantry and selflessness, served as a moral compass. They instilled in me a sense of purpose, a nudge towards embodying the qualities my father admired in Ferdowsi's Sohrab.

Later, I realized that being named after a hero wasn't about striving to meet an unattainable ideal; it was about reflecting the principles and spirit of what that hero stood for—acting with integrity, showing courage in adversity, and staying true to my values. My name, Sohrab, was more than just a link to mythic figures of the past, to heroes of old.

I also discovered that heroism comes in many forms, often quiet and unseen. In my life story, I encountered individuals who worked silently without thinking of their glory, embodying true valor through their quiet acts of sacrifice.

🐈 🐈 🐈

When my father, Mohammad, was nineteen, he journeyed to Istanbul, the Ottoman capital, and Russia, igniting his soul with liberal ideals and democratic fervor. He often recounted the significant impact of his visit to St. Petersburg in 1905, where the plight of the peasants and the cruelty of the Tsar's troops laid bare the glaring disparities of his world. These early voyages broadened my father's worldview. My mother, Massoumeh, on the other hand, led a more sheltered life, confined to a smaller world.

A fateful encounter unfolded long before either of my parents was born. In the late 1800s, Massoumeh's and Mohammad's families embarked on a camel caravan pilgrimage to the revered shrine of Imam Reza in Mashhad, in eastern Iran. During their sacred journey, the caravan was ambushed by Turkmen raiders spilling across the country's porous northern frontier. Although the raiders successfully plundered camels and treasures that day, the caravan's defenders mounted a valiant resistance. After a brief skirmish, they repelled the Turkmen, suffering no casualties.

Considering that many pilgrims fell prey to raids—where young women were often taken into slavery in the bustling markets of Central Asia—fortune had truly smiled upon them that day. United by adversity, the two families forged a lasting friendship and traveled together on subsequent pilgrimages for mutual protection.

Over time, this relationship deepened. Eventually, my mother's family moved from Isfahan to Qazvin, allowing their young daughter the opportunity to meet and get to know my father, who was ten years her senior.

However, Mohammad held firmly to one requirement for his future bride—she must be literate. This was the sole condition he set for his match-making parents, which reflected his forward-thinking spirit. This requirement led my father's parents to the doorsteps of Massoumeh's family home for *khastegari*—the Persian ritual of requesting a daughter's hand in marriage.

As they gathered in their living room, the air was thick with anticipation and the aroma of freshly brewed tea. Massoumeh served the tea gracefully and with poise, her movements like a delicate dance, adding to the room's warm, inviting atmosphere. An array of sweets and cookies adorned the table, each tempting to the eye.

During this gathering, Mohammad's mother, a woman of keen intellect and wit, expressed her admiration for one particular cookie. Curious, she inquired about its recipe and turned to Massoumeh's mother, her voice blending hope and sly intent.

"Could Massoumeh perhaps jot down the ingredients for me?" she asked, and Massoumeh eagerly agreed. When my grandmother returned home, she presented the neatly written recipe to her son. It was more than a list of ingredients; it was proof of Massoumeh's literacy, confirming her suitability per my father's sole condition. This simple piece of paper, scrawled with the recipe of a humble cookie, was the catalyst that transformed a traditional khastegari into the beginning of my parents' lifelong journey together.

Like many marriages of that time, their union wasn't built on shared interests. My mother, devoutly religious and superstitious, lived a life rich with pious ceremonies and pilgrimages to the shrines of her beloved saints.

My father, wary of her prolonged absences, restricted her spiritual odysseys to those within a few nights' journey to the local sanctuaries dotting Qazvin and its neighboring hamlets.

These rituals were her world, far removed from what my father loved: his business, reading poetry, and convivial gatherings where, to my mother's displeasure, the men sometimes consumed alcohol.

Unlike my mother, who revered the clergy, my father viewed them skeptically. He attributed superstition's proliferation among the people to their influence. He championed education as the cure for superstition, believing in the power of knowledge to dispel ignorance.

My mother's many travels meant that I was raised by servants, primarily by the same Fatima who was there at my birth and Haidar, our manservant. Haidar was a trusted confidant whose loyalty and kinship rivaled any blood relation.

The differences between Fatima and Haidar somehow symbolized the contrasting attitudes towards the changing world in Iran. With her unwavering superstitions and religious fanaticism, Fatima epitomized the backward ways that had been entrenched in Iran since the Arab conquest in the seventh century.

Fatima hung onto traditional beliefs and was wary of foreign influences, fearing that they would disrupt the sanctity of her way of life. She viewed the encroaching world with suspicion.

But it wasn't her fault. Women, particularly those of her social status, had few, if any, opportunities. Reza Shah's swift efforts to modernize Iran and promote women's rights, including access to higher education, were just beginning. One can't help but wonder if Fatima would have clung to her superstitions had she been literate and not solely reliant on the teachings from the mullah's Friday sermons.

On the other hand, Haidar rejected that restrictive and outdated mindset and did not desire to cling to old customs and beliefs. He represented a new breed of honorable young men who looked confidently toward the future and eagerly embraced the opportunities and advancements awaiting them.

Chapter 3

"It is difficult to free fools from the chains they revere."
Voltaire

Despite the chasm of belief between Fatima and myself, I was closer to her than to Massoumeh, who wasn't the warm, nurturing mother I craved. I don't recall even once when my mother hugged me. She cared so much about being pure for her prayers five times a day that she wouldn't allow me to sit on her bed.

Her stringent and unyielding devotion forbade even the slightest impurity from sullying her prayer to the extent that my presence, even at the edge of her bed, was deemed a contamination.

When I first asked her why, she explained with dispassionate clarity. "You piss standing up, and it splashes back on you, and you don't wash yourself. My prayers are nullified if anything unclean touches the bed I pray at."

It was no wonder that I never enjoyed conversations with my mother. This rigid barrier between us rendered any dialogue devoid of warmth. I often remember our talks becoming a religious lesson about something she believed I needed to be taught.

In contrast, I enjoyed my talks with Fatima. When I was a child, Fatima would sit with me whenever I was sick to keep me company, telling me about the adventures of her favorite Muslim saints. Because she was illiterate, she parroted the mullah's words from his weekly sermons.

Like clockwork, Fatima would start to cry whenever she mentioned her favorite saint, Hussein, a hero of the Shiites and grandson of the prophet Mohammad. Hussein and his followers were all massacred in Karbala, now in Iraq, by *kafars* (unbelievers).

My father once told me something interesting about our family's religious history, "Several generations ago, our family was Zoroastrian, the religion of ancient Persia. They were forced to convert to Islam with the threat of the sword."

Aware of my scant knowledge of Zoroastrianism, he shared the simplicity of their teachings. "The Zoroastrians believe in three main tenets: good thoughts, good words, and good deeds. That is all any religion needs; there is no need for more rules and regulations to burden the people," my father informed me.

In one of my conversations with Fatima, I told her of our family's Zoroastrian past, and she said, "Praise God that your family was forced to convert."

And then, with absolute conviction, Fatima reiterated her imam's teachings, declaring, "You know everyone is born a Muslim. It is their parents who mistakenly change their religion to something else."

Her confusing comment frustrated me, prompting me to challenge her: "Why do you pray in Arabic when you don't understand the language and cry for a saint from another country who died 1,400 years ago in some desert?"

"It's not for him that I weep," Fatima clarified, a softness in her voice.

"The tales of martyrdom make me sad, but it is the plight of my younger brother, Ismail, that makes me cry."

My curiosity was piqued, so I asked about Ismail's affliction. With emotion brimming, Fatima recounted an altercation between Ismail and their elder brother, Ibrahim, which resulted in Ismail losing part of his vision after a violent blow to the head with a chair.

Seeking solace and healing, they approached their local imam, known for his ability to write healing prayers. Fatima added, "When we arrived, we were told the imam was ill and was taken to the hospital, so we are waiting for him to get better. Once the imam recovers, we will ask him to help restore Ismail's eyesight."

I was astonished that Fatima couldn't see the absurdity of what she had just said — that the man they relied on for healing couldn't heal himself. Baffled by her answer and shocked by the sibling savagery, I shared the story with my father. He promptly made an appointment with an eye doctor for Ismail, and on the day of the visit, I tagged along.

During the examination, the doctor inspected Ismail's eyes, shining a light into them with a flashlight and a scope. After he was done, the doctor pulled my father aside and revealed a grim diagnosis: Ismail's vision loss was irreversible, a consequence of the head trauma. In the ensuing months, Ismail's world dimmed as he finally went blind.

One day, sometime later, I was in the kitchen with Fatima as she prepared dinner. I overheard her murmur something under her breath. When I asked her what she had said, she teared up and blurted, "Ismail is now blind because of the light the doctor shined in his eyes during the exam," completely dismissing her brother's violent act toward him.

When I heard that, I became irate, thinking how ungrateful she was, and asked, "Fatima, don't you remember you told me your brother Ibrahim slammed Ismail's head with a chair?"

She responded, "Yes, but that didn't blind him. He could see until then; right after the doctor shined the light in his eyes, he went blind. We also performed egg divination to identify the evil eye suspect. It turned out to be the eye doctor!"

I didn't know what egg divination was, so Fatima explained the superstition: "Whenever we suspect someone has *nazar-zadeh* (given the evil eye), we write the name of every possible suspect on an egg with charcoal. We also take two coins, put them on either side of the egg, and wrap them all in a cloth. Then, we press on the coins while reciting the suspects' names, and if the egg breaks, that person is the culprit. After Ismail went blind, we did the same, and when we said the doctor's name, *tokhme-morgh tarakeed* (the egg exploded)."

When I told my father what Fatima said, he urged me to see beyond her accusations, to understand the depths of ignorance and the lack of educational opportunities that ensnared women like her in a web of superstition. Sadly, at the time, the options were limited for women in Iran, especially for women like Fatima, whose duties were virginity, fertility, and obedience to men in the country's patriarchal culture.

A few weeks later, I ran into Fatima after a heated argument with my mother. She immediately noticed my agitation and wanted to know what was wrong. Frustrated, I asked, "Fatima, why does she behave like this?"

Caught up in my grievances, I failed to see Fatima's patience waning. She shot back cuttingly, "Maybe your mother acts this way because she's ashamed!"

Her comment was surprising. I demanded, "Ashamed of what?"

"Your mother tried to rid herself of you by leaping from the balcony the night you were born."

The words slipped from Fatima's lips before she could stop them. It wasn't in empathy that she said it. Fatima believed that my father's physician caused her brother's blindness, which made her resent me for telling my father. It was a difficult thing to hear.

"What? Are you saying my mother was so ashamed of me that she wanted to kill me before I was born? Ashamed of me, for what?"

Looking at my stunned expression, Fatima instantly regretted her indiscretion and disregard for her promise to my mother the day I was born.

Fatima stuttered, "No...no... Your mother's ashamed of how she tried to end it. She is ashamed of herself. Maybe whenever she sees you, her youngest son, her baby, she is reminded of her guilt and reacts that way!"

The weight of her revelation struck me hard. I never confided in my mother about Fatima's confession. I didn't feel close enough to ask her, and confronting her seemed impossible, which resulted in us growing further apart.

Desperate for answers, I turned to my father. The tension in the air was thick as he hesitated, a marked departure from his usual self-assuredness.

"That was when I was in Baku," he began slowly, each word weighed down by the gravity of the situation.

"I don't believe it. I asked Fatima about what happened, and she assured me your mother slipped and fell."

I wanted to believe my father, but his usually confident voice carried a trace of vagueness that mirrored my feelings.

In 1936, my mother stayed home for six months straight, not even going out once. She imprisoned herself in the house, announcing it was to protest the new *kashfe-hejab* (unveiling) edict proclaimed by Reza Shah.

This edict banned the *chador* (veil) and encouraged Iranians to adopt European dress. To enforce this decree, the police were ordered to physically remove the covering from any woman who wore it publicly. Women who refused were sometimes beaten, and their headscarves and chadors torn off.

This happened to Fatima, and she was humiliated. While in the bazaar, a policeman angrily ordered Fatima to remove her covering, threatening to remove it if she didn't. But she faithfully believed in the recent sermon of the local mullah, who had issued an ominous warning to the young girls at the mosque.

The mullah said that if even one strand of a female's hair is seen by a *namahram* man (a stranger or not a close male relative), she will go to *Jahannam* (hell). And while there, she will be hung by that same strand of hair above the blazing and ever-burning hellfire.

Fatima couldn't fathom being uncovered in public, so she didn't heed the policeman's warning and held on to her chador even tighter. She also gripped a piece of the covering with her clenched teeth to ensure it could not get separated.

But the policeman pulled it off her violently in front of onlookers. Embarrassed and distraught, she collapsed on the pavement, sobbing uncontrollably, drawing more attention to herself. This had a terrible psychological effect on her, as she never recovered from her fear of going to hell. From that day on, Fatima was not the same.

After hearing what happened to her servant, my mother couldn't imagine leaving the house uncovered. She probably thought it sounded better to say she was protesting while seeking refuge at home rather than going outside and suffering a similar public humiliation.

My last memory of Fatima was the day I was coming home from school and saw her run into the house, wailing and hitting herself on the head with both hands. Curious to know what happened, I asked Haidar.

He told me Fatima was washing her headscarf in the *joob* (the drainage ditch between the street and the sidewalk to carry water away) right in front of our house. Because this was her only headscarf, she draped the back of her shirt over her head to conceal her hair, heeding the mullah's caution of eternal damnation. But she was oblivious to the fact that this left her breasts exposed to all, including Haidar.

When Haidar alerted Fatima and told her to cover her chest, she looked down and realized what she had done. She screamed and cried loudly, *"Ay vay, khodaya, khak bar saram, hala meeram Jahannam!"* (Oh no, God, now I will surely go to hell!) convinced that a namahram seeing her two naked breasts deserves an even worse punishment than her showing a single strand of her hair.

Fatima locked herself in her room and refused to come out, no matter how much my parents tried to coax her, so my father called a doctor to come and examine her. His diagnosis was that Fatima was having a mental breakdown. Given her deep-seated convictions, the ordeal was too traumatic for her; no thanks to the mullah whose fiery sermon on hell ignited the whole thing.

My father contacted Fatima's family to inform them of the situation. Her relatives asked that we send her back to her ancestral village outside of Qazvin so they could look after her.

With Fatima gone, I naturally gravitated toward Haidar. He was older, with a life shaped by experiences far removed from mine. Haidar became more than just a servant—I would describe our relationship as "close as brothers," perhaps even closer than I was with my older brother, Arash, who had been sent to Europe years earlier to study and had not yet returned to Iran.

CHAPTER 4

"The lion who breaks the enemy's ranks is a minor hero compared to the lion who overcomes himself."

Rumi

Haidar came to work for my father years ago as a young boy and quickly became a part of our family. He was now a grown man: tall, handsome, and so beefy that he was called *pahlevoon* (champion or hero) in our neighborhood. His given name, meaning lion in Arabic, was a recognition of his bravery and strength. And he was a man of iron, a lion in human form.

Haidar's most meaningful association with his name came from his ingrained respect for Imam Ali, a saint revered by Shiites as a paragon of justice and honor to whom the name "Haidar" was famously attributed.

But beneath Haidar's imposing frame was a gentle heart and an insatiable thirst for knowledge. Haidar hailed from a small village amid the sweeping landscapes of the Zagros Mountains. His father was a farmer, and as the oldest son, it was assumed that Haidar would follow in his father's footsteps. But destiny provided another path for Haidar.

At an early age, he showcased an unquenchable curiosity that wasn't common among the children of his village. His passion for knowledge extended far beyond the confines of his small community. Haidar boldly questioned the elders and chased after the wandering merchants, eager to absorb their tales of distant lands, their stories a window into far-off realms.

Years back, during the Nowruz (Iranian New Year) celebrations, Haidar came with a merchant from his village to help carry wares to sell in the Qazvin bazaar. My father noticed the young boy's bright eyes and keen mind and offered him a position in our household on a whim. Haidar grabbed this opportunity, and what was supposed to be a temporary arrangement turned into a lifelong bond.

He had an infectious sense of humor and a unique way of viewing the world—finding joy and laughter in the simplest moments. I particularly remember one instance on a sunny afternoon as I walked home from school, the day I learned about microbes and diseases in class. I found Haidar sitting on a weathered wooden crate, taking a break from his usual chores. He was unwrapping his lunch—a generous portion of feta cheese in a thin cloth, accompanied by freshly baked Persian bread. I approached him as he took his first bite, seemingly savoring the cheese's salty tang.

But there were other plans for Haidar's lunch. As he leaned forward to take another mouthful, the cloth slipped from his grasp, and the precious feta cheese tumbled to the ground.

A nearby stray cat alertly darted forward, snatching the cheese in its jaws. Quick as lightning, Haidar leaped to his feet and chased after the nimble feline. Catching up to the cat, he instinctively gripped the animal's neck with a firm yet measured chokehold. The startled cat released the cheese, which landed with a splash into the joob.

Still holding the cat with one hand, Haidar plunged his other hand into the murky water, retrieving the fallen cheese without hesitation. It dripped and clung to his fingers, the remnants of the joob hanging stubbornly on its surface.

With a few swift strokes against his pants, he cleaned the cheese, undeterred by its less-than-ideal circumstances. He wasn't going to let a slight mishap ruin his meal.

He had such a firm grip on the cat's neck that I thought it would suffocate, so I pleaded, "Haidar, let the cat go!"

He replied, "But Sohrab Khan, no one takes my lunch unless I offer it."

Haidar laughed and let the cat go, telling me, "I wouldn't hurt it. I held onto him, trying to decide whether to keep it as a pet."

Then, as he was about to bite off a large mouthful of the disgusting cheese, I warned him, "Haidar, stop!"

He asked, "Why? I let the cat go. Just let me eat my lunch; I am dying to eat."

I told him that's not what I meant. "You could be eating microbes!" I exclaimed, trying to convey to him the potential dangers of what I just learned in science class.

Haidar paused, a puzzled expression crossing his face. "Microbes?" he repeated, the word foreign to his ears. I explained to him that microbes were tiny organisms that can cause illness but aren't visible to the naked eye.

He dismissed my concerns with a hearty laugh. "If it's so small that I can't see it with my eye," Haidar boomed, thumping his robust chest with pride, "How can it make me sick?" His laughter reverberated, carrying a sense of invincibility as he devoured the salvaged feta cheese.

But later that evening, Haidar sought me out, his earlier laughter replaced with a thoughtful frown. "Sohrab Khan, about those microbes…" he began hesitantly.

"Can they really make you sick, even if you can't see them?"

He was genuinely curious, trying to understand. "What do they look like?"

I retrieved my science textbook and flipped through the pages until I found an image of a microscope. "As I told you, we can't see them with our eyes alone," I explained, "but with this instrument, we can magnify them and see their true form."

Haidar took the book from my hands and focused on the picture.

"So," he asked, "there is a whole world out there, hidden from our sight?"

I told him, "Yes, like the stars at night. We can't see them during the day, but they're still up there, shining."

Haidar remarked with wonder, "Just because we can't see something doesn't mean it isn't there," his voice, filled with a newfound resolve, carried an eagerness to explore the unseen world revealed to him.

One day, I recall him confiding in my father about his ambition to be more than just a servant. Haidar wanted to be literate, understand the world, and compete with educated men. He believed that education could shatter the chains of servitude.

My father encouraged Haidar to pursue his dreams and helped him learn to read and write by enrolling him in night school. He was one of the few among his peers who was literate, which gave him confidence. Haidar took great pleasure in reading about the rich history and grandeur of the Persian Empire, and like my father, he was a patriot who deeply loved his country. He embodied a spirit of progress that was becoming more evident in men of his generation.

Though Haidar shared a similar social background to Fatima, the traditions that shaped their lives gave him a broader palette of opportunities, and he was aware of the significance of seizing them.

Haidar also carried a pocket watch, a gift for his graduation from night school. My father gave it to him as a symbol of the time he invested in himself and a reminder of his unyielding determination to grow. But more than his strength and intellect, his unwavering loyalty endeared him to us and bonded him with our family.

CHAPTER 5

*"The strong do what they can,
and the weak suffer what they must."*

Thucydides

Tehran, 1937

Eventually, my father's business prospects soared, and he became very wealthy. In 1937, like my mother, he also made a pilgrimage, but of a different sort, moving the whole family to Tehran to conduct his ever-expanding business from his favorite shrine, the main bazaar.

Haidar joined us, deciding to live in Tehran instead of provincial Qazvin. My father bought an estate with a mansion from a high government official, which became my childhood family home.

My father was an icon to me, and we were remarkably close. I cherished how he taught me things by telling stories or reciting Persian poetry. He loved poetry so much that he had calligraphers script Ferdowsi's poems and hung them on every wall of my bedroom. He told me I would begin memorizing the poems after looking at my walls for a while. After several weeks, the servants would change the calligraphed poetry. In this way, I memorized many poems from the Shahnameh.

My father mourned the darkness that had fallen over Iran, a land once vibrant and full of promise. He saw our country now ensnared in despair and hopelessness due to widespread poverty and inequality, leaving many disillusioned with the slow pace of progress.

In Ferdowsi's solemn reflections from the Shahnameh, my father saw a portrayal of Iran's ancient splendor fading into decay—a mirror of what we witnessed as our country suffered. A particular verse penned over a thousand years ago held fast in my memory.

This poem, which contrasted Iran's bygone majesty with the desolation the poet observed in his era, seemed to breach the barriers of time and place. It spoke to us, the descendants of those long-gone generations, reflecting our grief and longing for a glorious past. It was as if Ferdowsi transcended centuries to lament with us, his fellow Iranians, united in sorrow yet separated by millennia:

> *Where are your valiant warriors and your priests?*
> *Where are your hunting parties and your feasts?*
> *Where is that warlike mien,*
> *And where are those great armies that destroyed our country's foes? . . .*
> *Count Iran as a ruin, as the lair of lions and leopards!*
> *Look now and despair!*

Ahangar residence, Tehran, 1937

My father, an avid reader interested in global politics, profoundly shaped my sense of patriotism. He harbored a deep mistrust of the British and Russians, perceiving their historical involvement in Iran through the framework of the "Great Game" as both manipulative and exploitative. As a staunch nationalist, he despised these European powers for taking advantage of Iran's weakness, referring to them as bullies who used coercion to advance their geopolitical ambitions.

Anglo-Russian Treaty of 1907

This map shows Iran divided into two spheres of influence by the British in the south and the Russians in the north, with a third region between them as a neutral buffer zone. *(Image Source: "Division of Iran: Anglo-Russian Entente: August 31, 1907" from Iranreview.org)*

He often lamented the Europeans' hubris, particularly their insistence on calling our country Persia, what the ancient Greeks called our nation, rather than Iran, its rightful name.

"These Europeans are so arrogant," he would say, expressing frustration over the West's appropriation of our national identity. My father was especially critical of Winston Churchill, who preferred Persia over Iran to avoid confusion and only to distinguish it from Iraq.

I remember my father being ecstatic during our New Year celebration on March 21, 1935, when Reza Shah Pahlavi requested that foreign delegates use the term 'Iran' instead of 'Persia.' His emotions surged when discussing the matter, and he proudly declared, "Iranians no longer acquiesce to foreigners naming us what they want!"

He cautioned me about the British and Russians' ulterior motives: "They're aiming to maintain Iran's vulnerability to exploit our natural resources—the British eyeing our oil and the Russians desiring a warm-water port on the Persian Gulf. Unfortunately, we Iranians are too slow to recognize our enemies. It is not by an act of God that there is all this deprivation in our land. We could accomplish a lot if we could somehow slay these giants!"

One day, my father directed me to a framed editorial cartoon in his study, taken from the British magazine *Punch* and titled "*The Harmless Necessary Cat.*" I had seen the picture many times but never really paid any attention. The cartoon depicted the British lion and the Russian bear agreeing to manipulate Iran, represented as a Persian cat, without consent.

The caption read: British Lion (to Russian Bear): '*Look here! You can play with his head, and I can play with his tail, and we can both stroke the small of his back.*'

Persian Cat: *'I don't remember having been consulted about this!'*

My father detested the portrayal of Iran as a helpless animal, a docile cat, contrary to the lion symbolizing strength and pride on our national flag. "They view us as mere house cats, but we see ourselves as lions," he reminded me, emphasizing the disparity between foreign perceptions and Iranian self-image.

My father believed we needed a strong leader to have a chance at an independent Iran. The geopolitical landscape was fraught with danger, with powerful nations vying for influence in the region, and he feared that without a firm hand at the helm, Iran would fall prey to their ambitions.

"Even though Reza Shah is an autocrat and a dictator to some, he has begun transforming our country from its backwardness. He is lessening the mullahs' power, building a Trans-Iranian railway system, and allowing women to get an education. But I fear if the Shah acts too independently, these foreign powers will do away with him.

"Mark my words, son," he said, "The Europeans will seek to control our country if they cannot control our leaders. They know it's always easier to manipulate the leaders to get what they want. But if they can't influence them, they will look to start a war as a last resort. A war that will be costly and devastating."

I was young then and couldn't fully grasp his warning. I looked at him, nodded, and allowed his words to drift into the far corners of my mind.

In contrast to his distaste for the British and Russians, my father admired the Americans. He held American ideals in high regard, inspired by the Jeffersonian principles that certain liberties, such as religion, speech, and press, should be sacred to everyone.

It also helped that the American Revolution removed the yoke of British domination from the American people, something he wished for Iran. Most importantly, unlike the British and Russians, he viewed the United States as a benign emerging power, uninvolved in Iran's affairs. He once told me he thought I should attend university in America instead of Europe, where Arash had gone years earlier. But at the time, I wasn't thinking that far ahead.

🐱🐱🐱

My world turned upside down in 1938. I was thirteen when my father suddenly died of pneumonia. He was the center of my world, and his death left a deep void in my life. The shock hit me like a lightning bolt, sudden and jarring. One day, he was there, his larger-than-life presence filling our home, and the next, silence. A suffocating silence that consumed everything.

My mother, always reserved in showing affection, became even more distant and aloof following my father's death. Instead of coming together in our grief, she retreated into a shell, focusing solely on organizing my father's memorial service. Her world revolved around the logistics of death while I was lost in silent grief.

The nights were the hardest. In the darkness of my room, I'd lie awake, staring at the ceiling, yearning for a past that would never return. Memories of my father would play in my mind, a haunting reminder of what I had lost.

I felt completely out of place—I hadn't realized how much of my identity was tied to him. The security I once took for granted had vanished, leaving me unsure of myself. I felt disconnected without him, struggling to find my footing in a world that suddenly seemed foreign. I was left with countless questions.

As the days passed, the gap between my mother and me widened. Her priorities, anchored in rituals and remembrances, left no room for the raw pain of losing the cornerstone of our family. I felt I had lost both my parents—one to the clutches of death and the other to the cold embrace of indifference.

Chapter 6

"…A flickering flame that could never be brought into the light, forever destined to burn in the shadows."

Leo Tolstoy

Forty days after my father's passing, it was the *chehele* memorial, as they call it in Persian. Forty days are the usual length of mourning after the death of a family member or loved one in Muslim tradition. The house buzzed with activity, and family and friends gathered to honor my father's memory.

Sorrow draped itself over the room; tears flowed, and mournful wails erupted whenever the mullah recited prayers for the departed. But as soon as the sermon ended, the atmosphere shifted; the ceremony became a regular dinner gathering with an extravagant feast.

There was a disconnect between me and what was going on. The only thing I found worthy in the whole affair was that I knew the surplus food would be shared with the less fortunate as a charity, bearing my father's name.

My father never shared my mother's love of religious rituals and mournful gatherings. He often retreated from them to hide away in his study out of sight, only to emerge when the guests were long gone. I felt the same way on the day of his memorial.

But it was good to see my two older sisters, who had married a few years ago and moved to Masjed-Soleiman in southern Iran, where their husbands worked for the Iranian oil company. Despite their less-than-eager spouses, they made the trek to Tehran for the ceremony. But I had little in common with my sisters; they were older than I was and led lives more similar to my mother's than to mine.

The proceedings left me feeling strangely detached, as if I were observing from a distance rather than participating. So when I saw an opportunity, I seized it and, just like my father used to, quietly slipped away, seeking solace in the refuge of his study. Had I known the future, I would have cherished more time with my sisters. But in my grief, I sought solitude.

The room provided a respite from what overwhelmed me outside. It was as if the study's walls whispered tales of treasured memories and frequent talks my father and I had there, all now fading into the past. I roamed the shelves and examined the trinkets and mementos that decorated his desk, each holding a story of its own. The room was familiar but now foreign in his absence. As I searched the shelves and traced my fingers along the spines of his cherished books, I missed him terribly.

I then noticed the drawer where my father kept his diary. I reached for it, took it out, and flipped through its pages, admiring his meticulous and almost calligraphic penmanship. It was as if his soul resided within those inked words.

The diary witnessed my father's nightly ritual — the purifying release of thoughts and the recording of events that shaped his days. It mostly chronicled mundane affairs — a catalog of business dealings at the bustling bazaar and intriguing tales recounted by acquaintances.

As I continued to leaf through the pages, I stumbled upon a section titled *"Baku."* My father was on a business trip to Baku the night I was born in Qazvin.

As I read on, I unraveled a truth in this tranquil sanctuary. This entry held an intimate glimpse into my father's heart. He began it with a poem by Hafez, his favorite Persian poet, about a yearning for his lover. The verses flowed with emotion, capturing the essence of longing. Each line painted a vivid image of burning desire:

> *Hast thou forgotten when thy stolen glance*
> *Was turned to me, when on my happy face*
> *Clearly thy love was writ, which doth enhance*
> *All happiness? or when my sore disgrace*
> *(Hast thou forgot?) drew from thine eyes reproof,*
> *And made thee hold thy sweet red lips aloof,*
> *Dowered, like Jesus' breath, with healing grace?*
> *Hast thou forgotten how the glorious*
> *Swift nights flew past, the cup of dawn brimmed high?*
> *My love and I alone,*
> *God favouring us!*
> *I found Love's passionate wisdom hidden there,*
> *Which in the mosque none even now divine?*
> *The goblet's carbuncle (hast thou forgot?)*
> *Laughed out aloud, and speech flew hot*
> *And fast between thy ruby lips and mine!*
> *Hast thou forgotten when thy cheek's dear torch*
> *Lighted the beacon of desire in me,*
> *And when my heart, like foolish moths that scorch*
> *Their wings and yet return, turned all to thee?*

At the bottom, on the side, my father had added: *To my one love, Maryam.*

In his elegant, looping script, I found a dedication to his love, the ink on the page a keeper of his confession. My father, who made annual trips to Baku, had a life there that none of us knew about. His trips, it turned out, were not all business and no play; they also included clandestine liaisons with Maryam, his mistress.

The truth didn't shock me as much as it confirmed that my father and I had more in common than I thought. He and I both felt unloved by my mother. Her aloofness and emotional distance were not unique to me alone. My father sought comfort elsewhere, where he could find the tenderness and affection denied to him within our own home. I took his diary to my room; I knew no one would miss it. I continued reading it, curious to learn things about my father I didn't know.

The day after the ceremony, my mother's travel restrictions were lifted, now that my father wasn't around to keep her from visiting her favorite shrines. She immediately visited Karbala in Iraq to pray at the holy Shiite site there. She also undertook an extended pilgrimage to Mecca in Arabia, a journey she had longed to make for many years.

When she returned from Mecca, according to her wishes, no one called her by her name, Massoumeh, anymore. From that day forward, she even asked me not to call her 'Mother' but to address her by her newfound title, *Hajieh Khanoom* — a woman who had performed the hajj in Mecca.

The pilgrimage, however, took a toll unlike any she anticipated. In the holy city, amidst the throngs of the devout, Hajieh Khanoom fell ill. A severe case of cholera struck her, an illness rampant in Mecca due to the overcrowding and the limited sanitary facilities available to the vast number of pilgrims.

Upon her return to Tehran, weakened and frail, Hajieh Khanoom found herself confined to her bed, a mere shell of her former vitality. Her once energetic strides were now but a memory, as she could barely move without pain. But her faith remained unshaken. Each day, she would pray, sitting upright in her bed with great effort, her voice a murmur of devotion.

Chapter 7

"Of all the bad men, religious bad men are the worst."

C.S. Lewis

My older brother, Arash, who was in Germany studying, was informed of our father's passing by telegram. At my mother's insistence, Arash returned to Tehran to run the rudderless family business. Unfortunately, he didn't make it in time to participate in my father's cheheleh memorial.

I was excited that my brother returned home because he left when I was only nine. I idolized Arash and hoped he could fill the void left by our father's death. His time in Germany polished him, lending a sophisticated sheen to his persona. Arash embodied a worldliness that captivated my imagination as he spoke English and German and dressed like the movie stars I would see in magazines at the newspaper kiosk.

And to our surprise, he brought his new bride, Krista, a German woman from Munich whom he married shortly before returning to Iran. He kept the news from us, fully aware that our mother wouldn't be pleased when she found out.

Krista was a captivating presence with her elegance and delightful smile. Although she didn't speak Persian, we conversed in English, which I had learned in school. She even began teaching me German, and I appreciated the opportunity to practice.

Everyone was excited that Arash was married, except for our mother. Arash's assumption was correct; Hajieh Khanoom wore her disappointment like a heavy cloak. Her heart ached at the thought of her beloved son uniting with a woman who, in her view, had strayed from the true path of God.

Still, she found comfort in a single thread of commonality: at least Krista was not a pagan. For in the heart of the devout Muslim matron lay a begrudging respect for the 'people of the book.' Christians, after all, believed in God, even if their interpretation differed.

Arash coaxed Hajieh Khanoom to make Krista feel welcome, mentioning that if she saw how nice the Muslims in the family were to her, maybe Krista would convert. But Arash knew better; Krista would never renounce the faith handed down to her through generations; it was a compass guiding her.

In Tehran, Krista occasionally attended the prominent St. Sarkis Cathedral on Sundays, where other Germans in the community also gathered for worship. That first Christmas in Iran, she invited me to join her.

Inside the cathedral, the warm glow of candles illuminated the space, and the harmonious choir filled the air with Christmas hymns. The atmosphere felt worlds apart from the intense emotional rituals I had grown up with. While the Christmas service was a serene experience of light and song, it stood in contrast to the ceremonies of my youth, where an outpouring of communal sorrow and fervor swept through the streets.

Back then, I remember the streets transforming during the Muharram processions in our part of town. Wave upon wave of black-clad mourners paraded before us, their grief palpable and overwhelming. They rhythmically pounded their chests, a beat that underscored the somber mood. I recall feeling terrified by the passion play reenactments of the Battle of Karbala, their intensity blaring through the streets.

Some mourners even carried the physical imprints of their faith—marked by the self-inflicted wounds that wept blood from their foreheads, their backs etched with the scars of whips and chains. They engaged in a self-flagellation borne of a deep belief that inflicted pain, offering up uncalled-for sacrifices as if God was pleased when they suffered. As they marched through the neighborhood, the air filled with the sound of their lamentations, chants that pierced our ears, an eerie melody that fueled my childhood nightmares.

One evening before the Iranian New Year, Krista pointed to the *Haft-seen* table we displayed in anticipation of Nowruz. (*Haft-seen* is an arrangement of seven items whose names start with the letter "S" in Persian).

Items on our table included our Holy book, the *Qur'an*, a book of poetry by Hafez, the Shahnameh, a mirror and candles reflecting the future, a goldfish swimming in a bowl representing life, painted eggs symbolizing fertility, and all kinds of sweets and fruits.

"It's beautiful how your family celebrates," Krista remarked. "Back in Germany, we have our own traditions, especially around Christmas and Easter. Each carries deep meanings and rituals. The eggs you have on the Haft-seen table for your New Year are like the eggs we paint for Easter. We celebrate Easter for its promise of hope and renewal. It's similar to the rebirth theme of Nowruz."

Her mention of these German traditions sparked a new curiosity within me. I took our rituals for granted, viewing them as a part of our daily life. Still, Krista's perspective invited me to see them as vital threads linking us to our cultural and spiritual identities.

"What are your celebrations like?" I asked.

Krista's smile broadened, "Well, we go to church for Christmas, like when you came to St. Sarkis with me. Back in Germany, I attended church with my Oma. We were very close, and I miss her even more than my parents. After church, we gathered as a family, decorated our house, adorned our tree with candles and ornaments, and shared a festive meal. Oma used to read from the Bible, and we reflected upon the words."

I wasn't sure what her relationship with Oma was until she explained that *'Oma'* is the German word for grandmother. The similarity between our celebrations stirred something within me. For our New Year celebration, we also read from the *Qur'an* and recited the poetry of Hafez. Our traditions weren't so different after all, something I hadn't considered before.

Krista's voice softened as she spoke of her grandmother. This shift in her tone hinted at a well of emotions simmering beneath the surface. It was clear Oma loomed large in her life, even across the vast distance that separated them. As she spoke, I noticed a flicker of sadness, missing what she left behind in Germany.

"My Oma was a woman of great faith who wove her days with prayer and tradition. She'd attend our local church on Sundays dressed in her finest clothes."

As Krista spoke, I couldn't help but compare Oma's world to the one I grew up in. My mother, Hajieh Khanoom, was a pillar of our household, and her devotion to Islam was as intense as Oma's devotion to Christianity. But Krista's love for her Oma sounded different than my feelings for Hajieh Khanoom.

Krista sometimes read to me from her Christian Bible. Once, she showed me a hand-drawn family tree in the back of the book. "This, Sohrab," she began, her voice imbued with pride, "is not just a family tree. It's a journey through history." Her fingers paused over a particular entry, her touch almost reverent.

"See here," she pointed, her eyes meeting mine, "this is where I am connected to Martin Luther, a man of great importance in my religion."

Seeing my puzzled expression, she continued, "Martin Luther was a religious man, a monk, in Germany centuries ago. He challenged the prevailing powers of the Church."

I leaned in, intrigued to learn more. "How did this Luther challenge the church?" I asked. Krista excitedly shared, "He nailed his writings to the church's door, criticizing the Church's practices and corruption. His actions led to significant changes."

"But why is he so special to you?" I probed, sensing the deep respect she held for him.

"He stood up for his beliefs against immense pressure. His willingness to question and seek truth resonates with me. Having Martin Luther as an ancestor reminds me to be courageous and stand firm in my convictions," Krista explained, full of admiration for the man.

Before Krista shared her story, I had a simplistic view of Christianity, imagining it as a monolithic faith where all adherents believed in the same doctrines and practices. Her words painted a vivid picture of ideological upheaval. I listened carefully, absorbing the narrative of change and challenge. My mind began to draw parallels with our religious history and the division between Sunnis and Shiites, reflecting different understandings of Islam.

The Harmless Necessary Cat

I admit I was confused when she quoted verses about God's love instead of what I was used to: fear and eternal damnation for any religious indiscretion. In a household run by Hajieh Khanoom, we were always anxious that God was angry with us for all the good we were not doing and was ready to punish us for even the slightest misstep.

I still grappled with Fatima's tragic story. I shared with Krista how the mullah's words ensnared Fatima, plunging her into despair. She replied, "But Sohrab, it's not only here; peddlers of the word of God for profit are found everywhere. It's a sad reality that some use fear to control others. And that is precisely what Martin Luther was fighting against."

Krista sought to clarify the complex theological issues in terms that I could quickly grasp. "Martin Luther saw a big problem in the church. People were buying spiritual coupons, these pieces of paper, which they thought could reduce their punishment for sins, a shortcut to forgiveness."

She continued, "So-called holy men speaking of eternal damnation and insisting there must be strict adherence to a myriad of laws are in every religion. But that's not the God I know."

Her words reminded me of my father's cautionary tales about how some exploited believers' fears and superstitions to maintain control. I asked her, "Who is the God you know?"

She paused, searching for the right words. "The God I believe in isn't about a checklist of do's and don'ts to avoid punishment. It's about letting God take the lead in your life. You do your part, of course, but it's more about trust than fear. You can't earn your way to it."

I was glad to have Krista to talk to. It was liberating to discuss God and religion without being branded an unbeliever—a frequent consequence in my mother's eyes if I dared to probe too much.

Growing up, I viewed God as a stern judge, His wrath eclipsing His mercy, leaving me more fearful than comforted. That is why Krista's relationship with God was foreign to me. I was fascinated that she spoke as if she had a friendship with Him. Her perspective was different and warmer. Krista saw Him more as a close confidant, a friend to confide in.

"It's not about strict observance," she added. "The God I know isn't satisfied with bare, cold obedience. What parent would be content with slavish dutifulness without affection and confidence? He doesn't want you to try to be perfect so He can love you; he already does. That's how I see it."

At first, this notion seemed alien. How could someone regard the Almighty with such endearing familiarity? But the more I listened to Krista's tales of her faith, the more I transformed myself. Her words gently chipped away at the resistance I had built toward God, introducing me to the idea that perhaps He could be more than just a deity to fear.

🐈 🐈 🐈

The vacuum created by Hajieh Khanoom's illness allowed Krista to fill the role of the lady of the house. Our home began to shift under her influence, and the darkness cast by gloomy rituals slowly lifted.

As Krista took over the responsibility of running the household, she was acutely aware of the need to speak some Persian. So, she asked Arash to hire a private tutor and practiced with everyone in the house, myself included, at every chance. She even requested Arash to refrain from speaking German to force her to learn Persian.

Her dedication was incredible, and within a few months, Krista gained an impressive level of fluency. Her ability to grasp the nuances of the language, Persian culture, and customs endeared her to our family.

Transforming the home was no small feat, yet Krista executed it with grace and a distinctive European flair. Gone were the gatherings where lengthy verses and prayers droned in monotonous rhythms. The mansion bloomed anew with life.

She adorned the walls with tasteful European art, swapping velvet drapes for lighter, airier fabrics, all meticulously selected by Krista herself. The home that once resonated with religious hymns now vibrated to the harmonious strains of German cabaret, jazz, and classical music. It was a delightful transformation.

And we started having dinner parties. We had gatherings when my father was alive, but these were different. Arash and Krista's parties were a lively mix of men and women, their conversations punctuated by the clinking of glasses and the sight of guests lingering on the balcony for late-night drinks. As a teenager who had only ever seen such things in movies, I was captivated and loved every second of it.

What truly made these gatherings unforgettable for me was the grand reveal Krista had in store for her guests after dinner. She possessed a remarkable gift – her ability to recreate the luscious desserts of her homeland.

As a child, I wasn't particularly fond of Persian sweets, not because they tasted bad but because of the primary ingredient: *golab* (rosewater). Iranians have used rosewater in medicine, cuisine, and perfume since ancient times. The fragrant extract is produced by boiling

Damascus rose petals with water. The steam is then collected and condensed into a liquid in jars immersed in cold water.

My aversion to golab dates back to visits to holy shrines with my mother during religious holidays. All pilgrims had to remove their shoes before entering, and the odor was overpowering. Attendants would spray golab over the pile of shoes to mask the stench. But instead of covering it, the fragrance mingled with the smell, creating an even more unpleasant aroma that often left me queasy. As a result, the scent and taste of golab in Persian confections evoked the unpleasant memory of that pungent hill of sweaty, piled-up shoes.

But fortunately, I didn't feel the same about Krista's baked delights. It turns out her Oma wasn't just about piety. She told me her grandmother was also a formidable cook, her kitchen a haven of fragrant pastries, and that she had instilled a love of baking in Krista. I envisioned her grandmother as a seasoned baker in her kitchen, orchestrating a symphony of flavors, the air filled with the scent of cinnamon and nutmeg.

On the days of our dinner gatherings, when it was baking time, I would join Krista in the kitchen, watching her work. It was like witnessing an artist lost in her craft. She'd hum old German folk tunes, her fingers dancing gracefully over the dough, a look of sheer contentment on her face. There was undeniable magic in how Krista maneuvered around her kitchen, conjuring tantalizing German desserts straight from the heart of Bavaria.

With a soft sigh, she would begin by sifting flour, its snowy grains falling through the sieve, and dusting her apron. She'd glide her hands over a bowl of cherries as if she were selecting gemstones for a royal crown, each destined for her masterpiece: the Black Forest cake.

This was my favorite, and I felt lucky she liked baking so much. The cake stood like a majestic castle, tiers of chocolate sponge ensconced in whipped cream and punctuated with succulent cherries, as the kitchen filled with the intoxicatingly sweet smell of baking chocolate.

In Krista's sanctuary, time stood still, but outside the comforting confines of the kitchen, the world was quietly, inexorably transforming. We stood at the precipice of change, inching toward a future shrouded in the mist of the unknown. I recall those cherished moments within the kitchen's embrace as beautiful, fleeting pauses punctuating the ceaseless flow of time.

As the months passed, Hajieh Khanoom's health declined steadily. Her prayers became softer, and her moments of wakefulness fewer. Then, one quiet night, she passed away.

When Hajieh Khanoom died, I felt nothing. It was unlike the pain I felt the day my father died. As my family mourned her, I stood among them, feeling strangely detached from the grief. I watched Arash, tears welling in his eyes, and Krista, her face etched with sorrow. I wondered why my heart remained untouched. I had regret, not for Hajieh Khanoom's passing – for death is an inescapable part of life – but for my inability to grieve her loss.

Chapter 8

"Different cultures find different ways of expressing closeness."
Edward T. Hall

The economic uncertainty that gripped Germany after the Great Depression pushed many Germans to seek new opportunities abroad. Among the destinations they chose, Iran emerged as a land of promise.

The Iranian government, eager to modernize its infrastructure, sought technical assistance from Germany to build the Transnational Railway and develop its tele-communication systems. This call for expertise presented an appealing prospect for those seeking a fresh start. Thus, German citizens, drawn by economic opportunities and the allure of adventure, flocked to Iran.

Germans were involved in every aspect of the state, from setting up factories to building roads, railroads, and bridges, contributing to the growth of Iranian society. Their influence could be seen in the thriving German communities in Tehran, Isfahan, and Shiraz. German schools, clubs, and cultural institutions became integral to the Iranian landscape.

However, with the advent of the Nazi regime, these ties took on a new significance. The strategic location of Iran and its abundant natural resources made it an attractive ally for Germany, as it sought to secure vital supply lines and establish a foothold in the Middle East.

In the spring of 1939, Franz Mayer, a skilled German engineer, received an intriguing offer from the Iranian government. Iran needed foreign technical assistance to develop the country, and the Iranians highly regarded German expertise. The opportunity was tempting for Franz, and he embarked on a new chapter in his life, accompanied by his son Karl, leaving his estranged wife behind in Germany.

The close-knit expatriate community was a haven for Germans seeking solace and familiarity in a foreign land. They formed a tightly woven fabric of support, preserving their culture and traditions while adapting to the new surroundings.

In Tehran, German life took on a unique flavor. The community recreated German traditions, hosting events and celebrating their heritage. Even though the city's German community was relatively small, they formed a closely connected group that supported one another.

One prominent figure within this community was my sister-in-law, Krista. She was a vivacious and warm-hearted woman who brought the Germans together by hosting weekly gatherings and events at our house. These gatherings became a hub of friendship and camaraderie for them in Tehran.

The Mayers settled in Iran's lively capital, and the Germans already there welcomed them with open arms. As I used to address him, *Aghaye Mayer* (Mister Mayer) stood out for his towering stature and undeniable aura of elegance.

His features were chiseled, with a prominent jawline and piercing blue eyes that seemed to take in everything and miss nothing. His blond hair, peppered with a few strands of silver, was impeccably styled, and he moved with a grace that belied his size. He spoke several languages, seamlessly transitioning between English and German, and even spoke enough Persian to get by.

In Tehran's thriving German expatriate enclave, Mr. Mayer was a frequent topic of conversation. Women stole glances, hoping to catch his eye, and their quiet discussions revolved around his refined mannerisms. I'm not ashamed to say I was also captivated by his charm.

The weekly evening dinners Krista held at our home, which sometimes lasted until after midnight, were memorable. The servants set chairs and tables for the guests on the veranda above the ornamental pool. There was food, drink, and loud conversations as Marlene Dietrich's music played in the background on the gramophone Krista brought to Iran.

Krista told me her favorite of all Marlene's songs was "Falling in Love Again," which was performed in the 1930s film *Der Blaue Engel* (The Blue Angel). That is why Krista played the song frequently, almost to excess—so much so that I knew the melody by heart within a few weeks.

I particularly loved these gatherings, being the only kid around. It was a chance to see and hear things I wouldn't usually be privy to, especially since Arash and Krista didn't mind me sitting at the same table and having dinner with the guests. It contrasted with when my parents had people over; children were supposed to disappear. But with Krista's parties, it felt like the adults didn't even notice I was there. I was invisible, and it gave me unfettered access to their world.

The air at these soirees crackled with energy. I liked seeing how the foreign men and women enjoyed having fun as laughter and alcohol flowed freely. The guests could touch each other when talking, waltz shamelessly close, drink, and play card games together. But disapproving glances rippled through the room from the servants who viewed their closeness with disdain, especially while the foreigners indulged in forbidden alcohol. Initially, the interactions between the men and women shocked me. However, they were also fascinating, and I was caught up in the thrill of it all.

During one of those evenings, as the sultry tones of the German chanteuse filled the room, I found myself an unintentional voyeur on a curious exchange between Krista and Mr. Mayer. I saw her rise gracefully from her chair and saunter to him, who stood apart from the crowd with a frown marring his usually stoic features. Krista leaned in toward Mr. Mayer, and even though I couldn't hear their intimate conversation, they seemed engaged in playful banter.

🐈 🐈 🐈

"You seem to be the only one not enjoying Marlene's voice, Franz," Krista teased, sipping from her glass.

Franz straightened his posture. He looked Krista up and down as if taking in her full measure. "It is a pity that a woman who, like you, my dear Krista, is the essence of German femininity, would give up her German citizenship to become an American."

Krista raised an eyebrow, intrigued by his intensity. "It's just music, Franz. Besides, art knows no boundaries."

Franz scoffed, "It's not just about the music, Krista. It's about loyalty and principles."

She sighed, "Maybe Marlene didn't want to live in Germany, just like all of us Germans here in Iran, who decided to live elsewhere. People change, and so do their loyalties. Perhaps it's time you did, too."

Franz's demeanor suddenly changed. He paused momentarily, glancing around at all the guests, then back to Krista. A sly smile crept onto his lips as Franz winked and said, "Well, when you put it that way," his voice carried a newfound lightness, "considering you are the gracious host of this delightful evening, I suppose I can afford to be a bit more... accommodating."

Krista laughed, nudging him playfully, "That's the spirit, Franz! You never know; you might grow fond of the American's music."

Krista left to mingle with the other guests. While Marlene's haunting voice continued to serenade us, Mr. Mayer's gaze remained fixed on the record player, lost in his thoughts.

Arash came to talk to him, so I got closer to where they were situated, curious to hear them. I caught a little of what they said. Mr. Mayer didn't want to be overheard by the German guests as he spoke in Persian with Arash. His accent was thick, but he was surprisingly fluent.

Shoma deletan baraye Alman tang shodeh? (Do you miss Germany?), he asked.

Arash replied, "Studying in Germany was the highlight of my youth. If it hadn't been for my father's sudden passing, I doubt I would have returned to Iran. Krista and I have plans to move back once things settle down."

Mr. Mayer leaned in, "Arash, you seem to hold Germany very close to your heart."

"I do, Franz," my brother said with a tinge of nostalgia.

Franz nodded, "It's a beautiful country, tarnished only by current circumstances."

They moved farther away on the balcony, out of earshot, and I couldn't hear the rest of their conversation. Mr. Mayer looked around again, and I hid out of sight, worried he would see me watching them.

As they stood apart from the rest of the revelry, Franz continued his private discussion with Arash.

"You know, there are those of us who believe this tyranny under Hitler cannot last. There are…efforts…to ensure it does not."

Arash's interest was piqued, and he leaned closer. "Efforts? What kind of efforts?"

"I am part of a group…. we are a network of Germans from various backgrounds—aristocrats, intellectuals, even military officers. We share a vision for a Germany free from Nazi oppression, a Fatherland that values freedom and justice," Franz told Arash.

Arash, ever the idealist, was instantly captivated. "That sounds like the Germany I love and miss. But what can we possibly do from here in Tehran?"

Franz's expression hinted at hidden secrets. "There are ways, my friend, subtle yet impactful. We are gathering resources and funneling support through channels even the Gestapo hasn't sniffed out. Every bit of help counts."

Arash nodded slowly, his mind racing with possibilities. "And you believe these efforts can hasten the regime's fall?"

"I do," Franz affirmed with a quiet intensity. "And if you feel as strongly as you say about returning to a free Germany, perhaps there's a role you could play as well. Of course," he added quickly, "This is not a discussion for a crowded party. Let me caution you; speak of this to no one, not even Krista. Her connections, though innocent, include wives of Germans whose loyalties lie with the current regime. We cannot risk exposure. Let's meet soon, just the two of us, to discuss further." After they finished talking, Arash went inside, and Mr. Mayer remained outside alone, not rejoining the party. Krista returned, and the two walked closer to me, where I could hear what they were saying.

"You know, Franz, with that look on your face, sometimes I think you'd prefer if we were listening to Wagner instead of Marlene," she teased.

Mr. Mayer turned to her, a smirk playing on his lips. "Ah, Wagner stirs the soul, Krista. His music captures the spirit of our homeland, the grandeur of its history."

"Yes, indeed," Krista agreed, leaning against the railing. "So tonight, the time and place are for lighter fare, wouldn't you say?"

And with an inviting smile, Krista steered the conversation away from the earlier seriousness. "Well then, let's dance to whatever rhythm the night offers, shall we?"

🐈 🐈 🐈

There was something about how Krista and Mr. Mayer looked at each other as if they shared a concealed secret. I recall one evening when their laughter mingled over a seemingly innocent joke. Krista touched his arm lightly, her fingers lingering a moment too long. Their exchanges were peppered with coy glances and half-smiles, as if they existed in a secluded world, even amid the party's clamor.

During the lavish dinner that followed, they were seated side by side. As I clumsily passed a dish, my knife slipped off the plate and clattered to the floor. Bending to retrieve it, I noticed Krista's knee brushing against Mr. Mayer's under the table. It might have seemed accidental to the casual observer, but to my watchful eyes, it was deliberate.

Chance encounters became all too common. Once, I stumbled upon them on the veranda, where they spoke in hushed tones, their conversation charged with an undercurrent of something forbidden. Mr. Mayer helped Krista with her necklace, his fingers grazing the back of her neck in a fleeting caress. Both seemed acutely aware of the touch, the moment exposing the simmering tension between them. I couldn't shake the feeling that their attraction, masked as friendship, was becoming obvious. I wondered if anyone else had noticed.

As I watched this quiet interplay, a gnawing discomfort took root in my chest. Krista was, after all, my brother's wife, and the ease with which she gravitated toward Mr. Mayer unsettled me.

I often dismissed these observations as a cultural familiarity I might not fully understand. They were both German, far from their homeland, and perhaps this shared heritage forged a merely platonic kinship, a semblance of closeness born of similar memories and a shared language. I explained away each laugh, each seemingly innocent touch, as a facet of their German camaraderie.

I thought, *Perhaps this is just how they are. Maybe in Germany, such displays are commonplace among friends.*

This reasoning provided a fragile peace of mind. I was loath to consider the alternative—that Krista and Mr. Mayer might have a more intimate relationship. I hoped that what I perceived was nothing more than a friendship strengthened by the common bonds of a distant home.

Arash, a gracious host and seemingly oblivious, showed no signs of discomfort with their interactions. My brother was remarkably friendly towards Mr. Mayer, often clapping him on the back or sharing a hearty laugh over a glass of schnapps, a taste he acquired during his time in Germany.

Arash was not shy about displaying affection, either; he was equally warm and engaging with the women at our gatherings. His easy flirtations and open smiles mirrored the behavior I noticed in Krista. My brother and his wife behaved in much the same way, which eased my doubts.

Perhaps this was how things were done in our cosmopolitan Tehran bubble. The city was a fusion of various influences, with people expressing themselves far more freely than I was used to. Seeing Arash so at ease and unfazed by it all reassured me.

The music, the laughter, and especially the open displays of affection at those gatherings made me feel alive. It was all so exciting and new, as if I'd stepped onto the silver screen, reliving a scene from one of the films we'd seen together at the Homa Theater.

The last time we went was to watch Marlene Dietrich in *The Blue Angel*. Before the film began, a flickering *Pathe'* newsreel showed war erupting in Europe. Hitler's forces had just invaded Poland. For me, it felt distant, a conflict unfolding on a faraway stage. But it was different for Krista, whose birthplace – Germany – lay at the heart of the storm. I could see how the weight of the news affected her. Maybe when she left Germany, Krista thought she'd outrun Europe's war. But now, the war followed her like a menacing specter breathing down her neck.

A curious kinship bloomed between Iranians and Germans during this tense period. Both harbored a deep-seated resentment towards British imperialism. For decades, the British had exploited Iran's strategic location and rich oil reserves, fostering a simmering anger among the Iranian people.

Unlike the British, Germany lacked a history of direct colonialism in our region. This fact and the booming trade between our two nations fostered a certain allure. In 1939, Germany became Iran's top trading partner, accounting for nearly half of our total trade.

As news of Germany's advances in Europe and its confrontation with the British spread, we found ourselves intrigued by a country that dared to challenge British supremacy. We saw Germany as a nation that defied the odds and resisted the encroachment of colonial powers, forging a path to greatness. We Iranians hoped for a change in the geopolitical landscape, freeing us from the clutches of foreign domination.

Many in Iran saw Germany as a potential liberator, a power capable of breaking the stranglehold of foreign influence. They viewed a tactical alliance with Germany as an opportunity to elevate Iran's status on the world stage. This alignment was not rooted in shared fascist ideology with Nazi Germany but rather in a strategic effort to counterbalance British and Russian dominance. Others, however, remained cautious, fully aware of the perilous nature of wartime alliances.

Chapter 9

"The world is a vast hunting ground, and we all seek our prey. But are we the hunter or the hunted?"

Sa'adi Shirazi

A decade earlier, in the 1930s, the German colony in Tehran had opened a school for German-speaking children, where Mr. Mayer's son Karl now studied. The school, an imposing structure built in the architectural style of the time, stood at the city's edge, surrounded by gardens that thrived despite the arid climate. It served as a place of learning and as a gathering spot for the small German community in Tehran.

Karl attended classes there but remained distant from the nationalistic zeal that infused parts of the curriculum and some of the teachers' beliefs. He was more interested in the literature and science classes, showing a keen interest in the world beyond the ideologies gripping his homeland.

I first met Karl when he and his father visited our home one afternoon soon after they arrived in Iran. Just as I was eager to learn more about Europe, Karl also appreciated my native insights into Iran, which were equally unfamiliar and fascinating to him. Our friendship blossomed from a shared curiosity about our contrasting worlds, and we eventually spent most of our free time together.

With striking blue eyes, blonde hair, and a naturally tall and handsome stature, Karl embodied the Aryan ideal that was so celebrated in his homeland at the time.

He was a couple of years older than me and taught me a lot about the world beyond Iran's borders. Little did we know that the events unfolding in Europe would shape our lives in ways we could never have imagined.

While the drums of war grew louder, the world edged closer to a conflict that would soon test the bonds we had formed. But, in the heart of Tehran then, such concerns seemed distant as we reveled in our camaraderie.

Karl's father was frequently away on business trips, involved in projects for the railway system that was part of Iran's rapid modernization. When Mr. Mayer remained in Tehran, he took trips with Karl to hunt in the mountains north of the city, sometimes combining his inspection work with a weekend retreat.

Karl loved wearing his most treasured possession on these hunting trips, a Persian lamb coat crafted from exquisite fur his father gifted him upon their arrival in Iran. He adored the coat so much that he wore it at every opportunity. It clung to his frame like a second skin.

Karl and Mr. Mayer visited us the day before one of their trips as Karl wanted to show me something. Earlier that morning, his father handed him a rifle he had brought from Germany, a Mauser, a relic from the German engineering prowess of the 1930s. Karl was eager for me to see it.

Crafted with precision, the Mauser paid homage to both history and artisanship. It was a bolt-action rifle used extensively during the First World War and had a rich heritage in European hunting circles. Karl and I went outside to test the weapon.

"I've been practicing with my father's rifle since I was twelve, you know," Karl confided, his fingers tracing the polished wooden stock of the firearm. He had a way with the weapon, almost second nature. I watched in awe as he quickly dismantled, cleaned, and reassembled each part that afternoon. I asked Karl how he learned to do that.

He replied, "My father taught me. He told me this rifle was engineered for straightforward maintenance and that German soldiers were routinely trained in basic field stripping—disassembling it quickly and without specialized tools."

"Impressive, but why do you hunt? I don't like the idea of killing animals like that," I blurted out. The thought of taking an animal's life for sport sat uncomfortably with me.

Karl took a deep breath, "Sohrab, let's be honest, I have already seen the barbaric street side butchery of sheep for your religious occasions here. Some guy is hacking away at the poor animal's throat, and blood is gushing into the joob. That's hard to watch. I think a bullet is probably more humane."

He trailed off, lost in thought, then continued, "Truthfully, though, the reason I like these hunting trips isn't for the kill but to spend time with my father. With his travels for work, these trips are some of the only moments we share. It's… special."

The way Karl idolized his father was heartwarming and made me miss my father.

"Would you like to try it?" he suddenly offered. Karl held out the Mauser, urging me to overcome my reservations. I hesitated but then accepted the rifle. My hands felt awkward holding it. The weight was more substantial than I had anticipated, and for a moment, I was fully aware of the power in my grasp.

While Karl stood beside me, his hands expertly guiding my posture and aim, I developed a newfound respect for the skill required. My fingers gingerly curled around the trigger as we adjusted the sight, aligning it with a bottle in the distance. As I practiced, I focused on the weapon's mechanical precision and balance, momentarily setting aside thoughts of its deadly purpose. I could almost understand the allure it held for Karl.

I had no idea that soon, as Hitler turned his gaze eastward toward the Soviet Union, countless German soldiers — only a few years older than us — would feel the same weight of their Mausers as they hunted Russians like prey on the Eastern Front.

Part II: The War Years

PART II THE WAR STARS

CHAPTER 10

"War does not determine who is right - only who is left."
Bertrand Russell

Tehran, 1941

The stunning German victories reverberated across the European landscape, and the Allies were determined not to let the dominoes fall. Iran became the stage for their grand maneuvering. It was a tale of hidden agendas, strategic calculations, and the tenacious pursuit of victory.

In the summer of 1941, the Germans launched Operation Barbarossa, their assault on the Soviet Union. The campaign was named after Frederick Barbarossa, the 12th-century German king and Holy Roman Emperor who sought to establish German predominance in Western Europe.

In response, a secret plan brewed within the corridors of power in London and Moscow. The newly allied British and Russians demanded the Iranian government expel all German nationals from Iran, which Reza Shah declined twice, citing Iran's neutrality in the war and stating that the Germans in Iran had nothing to do with the Nazis.

The British pressured the Shah, which increased tensions and anti-British rallies in Tehran. London viewed these protests as pro-German rather than anti-British, attributing them to German propaganda or agitation instead of recognizing the genuine grievances of the Iranian people against British interference.

With the king's refusal to remove German citizens from Iran, the British and Soviet governments seized this opportunity to occupy the divided nation. Deep down, they feared that the unstoppable German war machine would not halt at the Iranian border, posing a dire threat to their strategic interests. They saw Iran's neutrality as an obstacle hindering the flow of supplies from British India to Egypt and the lifeline of British supply routes to the Soviet Union.

Moreover, the ostensibly impartial Reza Shah was seen as difficult to control and possibly suspected of sympathizing with the Nazis. The British and Soviet governments agreed that merely attempting to exert influence over Iran would not suffice. Just over two months following Hitler's Operation Barbarossa, the Allies initiated Operation Countenance, the invasion and occupation of neutral Iran.

In the early morning of August 25, 1941, a strange and ominous feeling filled the air as dawn broke over Tehran. The rumors had been swirling for days — the Allies were coming and bringing war with them. World War II had brought the conflict to Iran's doorstep, and now the capital city was about to experience the wrath of foreign powers.

The silence of the morning was broken by a strange buzzing sound that grew louder and louder. My heart pounded in my chest as I scanned the horizon. I was shocked to see a formation of what turned out to be British Royal Air Force (RAF) aircraft flying overhead, their looming silhouettes against the morning sun.

The invasion had begun.

The planes were swift, darting through the sky like predators searching for prey. As they flew over Tehran, they dropped leaflets written in both Persian and English. The message they delivered to the people of Tehran was that the Germans were planning to invade and that we should evacuate the city. The leaflets also urged us to support the Allied forces.

It was a strange and perplexing sight, as Germany and Iran had no formal alliance, yet our fate seemed intertwined. The leaflets urged us to remain calm and cooperative, promising the Allied forces were there to protect us from the Germans.

It made no sense to me, and most Tehranis felt the same. The Germans were helping build our country, and my dear sister-in-law, Krista, and Karl, my best friend, were German. So, these Allies were invading our homeland to protect us from people like them? We didn't ask for this imposed protection. Germany had never invaded or occupied Iran, so why would we be worried about them?

As I wondered why the Allies were dragging the mess of their European war with Germany onto my country's doorstep, I remembered the time my father had cautioned me about Russian and British selfish interests in Iran. Back then, I didn't take his warning seriously. I thought it was just the concern of an aging man. But he was right, and his words replayed in my mind, a clear reminder that some warnings are never genuinely heard until it's too late.

The atmosphere in Tehran was tense. The aircraft engines reverberated through the streets, creating a dissonant symphony that played on our nerves. Fear gripped us, and we sought refuge in our homes, unsure of what the day would bring. Then, without warning, the leaflets were replaced by bombs. The British planes unleashed their payload on select targets across the city, transforming the tranquil neighborhoods into scenes of destruction. Plumes of smoke and debris now marred the once-peaceful urban landscape.

My cousin Abbas contacted us from Qazvin to see how we were holding up, informing us that his house had a direct hit and was damaged by RAF bombs. The Allies came with a promise of protection, but their bombs were indiscriminate. As the explosions shook the ground beneath us, we couldn't help but wonder if there was any truth to the assurances in those leaflets.

In Tabriz, Ardabil, Mashhad, and Rasht, the Soviet air force dropped similar leaflets written in Persian and Russian, warning of the German threat, followed by the unforgiving wrath of their bombs. The civilians and residential areas bore the brunt of these attacks, leaving behind trails of destruction. Countless lives were lost, and more were left wounded and broken.

Soviet T-26 Tank driving through Tabriz, Iran, August, 1941

In addition, Russian and British ground troops simultaneously launched a coordinated assault on multiple strategic locations throughout the country. The Allied military leaders meticulously planned their joint operation, which had multiple goals within this clandestine effort.

One objective was safeguarding the precious British-controlled oil fields, which became paramount, for the Allies knew that controlling Iran meant securing a source of immense power. Another aim was to utilize the Trans-Iranian Railway, a pathway they named the "Persian Corridor," to transport military supplies to the beleaguered Soviet Union.

This lifeline to the Soviets was crucial, connecting Tehran with the Persian Gulf to the south and the Caspian Sea to the north. It was also the most efficient route available. This corridor was strategically important now that the once safe Arctic convoys plying the treacherous waters to the Russian port of Arkhangelsk encountered a new menace—German U-boat attacks that prowled the frigid seas.

The Allies knew the brutal winter conditions would challenge even the most daring naval missions. Therefore, they needed an alternative, a safer and more reliable way to supply the Soviets. The Trans-Iranian Railway was a sturdy pathway snaking through Iran's rugged terrain. Its potential as an essential corridor became evident as the U-boat attacks escalated, choking the supply lines to the Soviet Union. So, the focus shifted to this land passage through Iran—one that could make a decisive impact on the war's outcome.

Another motive lurked in the background of the Russian and British incursion—an urgent need to thwart the cunning German intelligence activities in Iran, which threatened to unravel the Allies' intricate plans.

Allied Forces Sweep on in Iran (August 1941)

Map legend shows the origins and direction of Russian and British attacks as the two nations invaded Iran. They asserted it was to protect oil fields from sabotage by German agents they claimed had infiltrated there. (*Image Source: Iowa City Press-Citizen Newspaper Archives August 26, 1941*)

British army supply convoy headed by Soviet BA-10 armored vehicle, Iran, September 1941

As news of the invasion spread, there was widespread confusion and fear among the people. The British and Russian combined forces faced minimal resistance without any coordinated Iranian defense. Iranian forces, caught off guard and ill-prepared for such an attack, were quickly overwhelmed by the combined might of the invaders.

Amidst the chaos, our king, Reza Shah, made an unexpected decision. Panicked by the swift invasion, his generals urged him to destroy the road and transportation networks to hinder the advancing Allies.

But Reza Shah hesitated. He had painstakingly built the infrastructure during his reign, and the thought of causing irreparable damage to his creation troubled him. Ultimately, his decision inadvertently paved the way for the Allies' rapid victory. With no allies and facing massive defeats, the Shah ordered the Iranian military to stop fighting and stand down on August 29, four days into the invasion.

The invasion left the Iranian military and government in disarray. Reza Shah, already facing internal opposition and pressure from both sides, was forced to abdicate in favor of his son, Mohammad Reza Pahlavi.

Once again, my father proved remarkably prescient in predicting that the British and Russians would try to eliminate a strong-willed leader like Reza Shah because a weak Iran was in their interests.

The capture of Tehran, our beloved capital city, dealt a severe blow to the Iranian leadership. The attack marked the first successful collaboration between the British and Soviet forces during the Second World War, setting a precedent for future joint operations. The invasion of my country fomented resentment and anti-Western sentiment among many, who saw themselves as victims of imperialistic ambitions. The occupation further intensified the divide between Iran and the Allies, foreshadowing the tumultuous relationship that would persist long after the war's end.

Chapter 11

"What is time?
Hidden in the silence of the celestial sphere,
no one knows the secret of this magic spell."

Manuchehri Damghani

My evenings in Tehran were often spent under a clear sky, eyes cast upwards, tracing the pathways of constellations, musing over the celestial puzzles that once challenged ancient astronomers. This was precisely why timepieces fascinated me; they were not just tools for measuring time but bridges to the eternal dance of the cosmos.

As I grew older, my fascination with time only grew stronger. I often asked my father about the history of timepieces, and he indulged my curiosity by sharing books that detailed how humans began measuring time. These books, filled with tales of sundials and intricate clockwork, became my treasures.

A few months before my father died, on the eve of my thirteenth birthday, he handed me a small, velvet-lined box, its contents a mystery that only heightened my anticipation.

"I brought this back from Baku," he said, his voice rich with nostalgia. "I thought it would make the perfect birthday gift for you."

My heart raced excitedly as I carefully opened the box, eager to discover what lay inside. The box, unlike its contents, held no trace of luxury. Inside, nestled on a bed of faded crimson, lay a pocket watch. Its face, a labyrinth of Cyrillic script and looping hands, spoke of a different world - a world of czars and samovars, a world my father had glimpsed on the fringes.

My father explained, "It's a Russian pocket watch crafted by the First Moscow Watch Factory. Baku is a vibrant city, and one can find many fine things there, including this timepiece."

The watch was heavier than I expected. As I held it delicately, feeling the steady ticking and smooth, cold metal against my skin, I imagined the watch's journey — from the bustling factories of Moscow to the vibrant streets of Baku and, finally, to me in Tehran.

The timepiece became more than just a birthday gift from my father; it was a link to a world far beyond my own. But despite the pocket watch's undeniable elegance, a small part of me yearned for something different. As much as I treasured the pocket watch's old-world charm, a nagging desire for a more modern watch tugged at me.

First Moscow Watch Factory, 1SWF Pocket Watch Caliber: K43 (7 Jewels)

A wristwatch's practicality and sleek design held a certain allure, a promise of effortless timekeeping that the pocket watch, a relic from another era, in all its beauty, couldn't quite fulfill. A wristwatch would be a welcome change, freeing me from the constant dance between pocket and palm.

My father placed a hand on my shoulder, his voice filled with wisdom.

"Time is a precious gift," he said softly. Then he recited a verse from the Persian poet Omar Khayyam:

"Be happy for this moment. This moment is your life."

He looked at me, his face revealing the undeniable truth behind his words. "Remember, my son, every moment we live is fleeting. Cherish each one, for they pass quickly and cannot be reclaimed."

Growing up with an Iranian father, I was used to hearing him recite poetry to convey his advice and sometimes his warnings. In Persian culture, poetry is a medium for expressing deep philosophical and spiritual truths. Fathers often use the verses of poets like Rumi and Hafez to communicate important life lessons, wrapping their guidance in the beauty of lyrical language.

Over time, the frequent recitation of verses became a comforting routine. The advice and knowledge embedded in the poems often faded into the background, leaving me to savor the sweetness of the words and the melodic rhymes.

I could recite many of them by heart, having heard them countless times. However, because they were repeated so often, I usually missed the more profound meanings beyond the beauty of the verses.

When my father passed away suddenly just months later, Khayyam's lesson became painfully clear—time, once lost, slips beyond our grasp, leaving only memories in its wake.

🐱🐱🐱

A few weeks after the initial occupation of Iran, a sense of normalcy began to emerge from the chaos of the invasion. On a Friday, the start of the Iranian weekend, I persuaded Karl to join me for a visit to the *hammam omumi* (a public bathhouse) just a short walk from our home. While he was accustomed to the German tradition of saunas and spas, Karl was excited to immerse himself in this deeply rooted Persian tradition. He had heard stories of ancient Iranian bathhouses — communal spaces where people cleansed their bodies and exchanged news and stories while enjoying the soothing warmth.

Karl came over, and we set out toward the bathhouse. As we walked on, I was drawn to a magnificent timepiece on Karl's wrist. It was a Flieger chronograph — a showcase of impeccable German craftsmanship.

"Karl, that watch is incredible. Where did you get it?" I asked, unable to hide my admiration.

A smile broke across Karl's face, "My uncle, a pilot in the Luftwaffe, gifted it to me when we left Germany for Iran," he explained nostalgically. "He said that it would remind me of home whenever I used it to check the time."

I was intrigued by Karl's watch and by the concept of time itself. I considered myself passionate about learning all I could and felt quite knowledgeable about the subject. I also didn't mind showing off when the topic of time came up, especially since most of my peers either didn't know or didn't care about it.

That's why I asked Karl, "Did you know that my Mesopotamian ancestors were pioneers in timekeeping?

They divided an hour into sixty minutes and a minute into sixty seconds. Ever wondered why sixty, not ten or a hundred?"

Karl seemed interested and said, "Yes. I have wondered why. Why not something straightforward like the metric system—tens and hundreds, like our money, or the measures we use like meters and liters? And why twenty-four hours in a day?"

I chuckled softly. Having lived in Germany, Karl knew so much about different topics. I hadn't thought I could offer anything interesting in return, so I jumped at the chance to repeat what my father had told me.

"The skywatchers of the past believed the heavens mirrored their world. With twelve lunar cycles marking the year, the number twelve became sacred. So, twenty-four hours mirrored the balance of day and night."

"That makes sense," Karl glanced at his watch again as if seeing it in a new light. "But why sixty for the hours and minutes? Why not a hundred, as you mentioned?"

I told him, "I also once asked my father the same thing; he said he didn't think anyone knows but told me it may be because the beauty of sixty lies in its divisibility."

I was excited as I shared the information with my friend, eager to see his reaction to something he probably hadn't heard before.

"Sixty can be divided by twelve different numbers. This made it incredibly useful for calculations and creating a calendar aligned with the planets they observed nightly. They needed a system of timekeeping for more precise predictions for their agriculture practices and religious observances," I told Karl.

I was confident I had conveyed my father's wisdom almost verbatim. Karl remained silent for a few seconds, then raised an eyebrow and asked, "So, if you're such an expert on time, tell me—do you know why exactly we have seven days in the week?"

He posed the question with a triumphant smirk, and I was totally caught off guard. I assumed my father had well-primed me for such inquiries, but I had never asked him this. Sometimes, we overlook the most obvious questions.

Knowing he had outsmarted me, Karl leaned in and matched his smirk with a smile. "I'm surprised you didn't know. Wouldn't that be one of the first things you would be curious about if you are fascinated with time? Why are there seven days in a week? Why not ten, for example?"

He paused, making sure he had my full attention. Meanwhile, my earlier confidence was now replaced with rapt curiosity.

"The same Mesopotamian ancestors you just told me about venerated the number seven, which held divine significance for them. They observed the moon's four-quarter phases; seven days closely corresponded to each phase. Another is that what was visible to the naked eye were the Sun, the Moon, and five planets, which make seven. That's how the week was born."

In my eagerness to impress, I had underestimated Karl, mistaking his quiet demeanor for ignorance when, in fact, there was hidden depth. He knew far more than I had given him credit for, and I humbly realized I wasn't as knowledgeable as I had assumed.

While listening to him, my eyes were fastened on his watch as he gently ran his fingers over the smooth surface of the timepiece, tracing the contours with tender reverence.

Deep inside, I coveted his watch and wished it was mine. Still staring at it, I blurted out, "Your uncle gave you a great gift to remember him by; the watch connects you to your home and the heavens."

The mention of his uncle brought out a seriousness in Karl that contrasted with his earlier jovial mood. "The war between Germany and Russia is escalating, my friend," Karl began, he said with anguish. "My mother wrote to me recently…"

Until then, Karl hadn't told me about his mother, seemingly reluctant to divulge much. But I was curious about her and hoped he would tell me more. Now that he mentioned her, I saw an opening.

I asked him, "What's her name?"

He said, "Helene."

I continued to probe, "Why didn't Helene come to Iran with you and your father?"

Karl, at first unwilling, slowly began to tell me about her. "Well, she is a morally conscious and sensitive woman, and the changes unfolding in Germany were unsettling for her. She was disturbed by the atmosphere of fear and oppression brought about by the Nazi regime. She was always so spirited."

Karl didn't answer the question, so I impatiently asked, "If she didn't like it there, then why didn't she come with you to Iran?"

As Karl continued his story, his hesitation became evident, as though he was skirting around something uncomfortable. He avoided discussing the reason for Helene's absence, instead shifting the focus to one of her friends.

"Back in Germany, she had a friend, more like a sister, Sophie; they were so close that I used to call her Aunt Sophie. She was part of a small group of students at the University of Munich. They considered themselves a resistance group that was mailing leaflets to people in

Munich, denouncing the Nazi regime, and they spoke out forcefully, condemning the moral indifference and apathy of the German people."

I asked, "Indifference and apathy to what?"

"To the suffering," Karl said. "To the atrocities. What is happening in my country is not right. I remember my mother talking with Aunt Sophie for hours about the future of Germany. She believed in their cause and respected her friend for not standing idly by while injustice unfolded. But she also constantly worried for her safety.

"My mother told me that she once asked Aunt Sophie if she feared what the Gestapo might do to her. Sophie told her, 'You have to stand up for what you believe in, even if you stand alone. An end in terror is preferable to a terror without end.'"

"The who?" I interrupted, unfamiliar with the term.

"The Gestapo," Karl repeated, his expression darkening.

"They are the secret police of Nazi Germany, ruthless and unforgiving. They hunt down anyone who opposes the regime, anyone who dares to speak out or resist; that's why my mother was worried for her friend. She said their leaflets offered hope amid despair. But my father saw it differently. He thought their approach was reckless and would only bring more suffering. He believed a handful of students with pamphlets couldn't solve the country's problems. My parents didn't see eye to eye on the matter."

I asked, "Your father never spoke about this with you?"

Karl shook his head. "He wouldn't. To him, it was a private matter. He always said politics should stay out of family affairs. But despite that, I did hear him warn my mother to stay away from Aunt Sophie for fear of her getting mixed up in things that would mess up his career."

"It sounds like your father was more concerned with his position than what was happening in Germany," I said.

"Yes, that's exactly it. My father couldn't see past his ambitions," he confessed.

Karl still hadn't offered a reason for Helene not joining them to come to Iran, so I asked again, with a tinge of frustration, "So why didn't she come with you?"

He reluctantly replied, "A few months before we left Germany, something happened; I don't know what it was, but she withdrew. Her attitude suddenly changed, and her relationship with my father became strained. I sensed a rift between them, Sohrab, a tension, but nobody talked about it. I... I never really understood it. It's all a bit of a haze now, mixed with too many feelings."

There wasn't anything I could say, so I nodded and listened, offering him my full attention. Karl continued, "It was sad when I said goodbye to my mother...I remember feeling confused. I kept asking her why she wasn't coming with us, but she told me she wasn't getting along with my father, and they needed some time apart. I hope for my parents' reconciliation at some point. Maybe being away for a bit will help them miss each other."

His voice cracked slightly when he spoke of his parents' separation. My heart ached for him; however, from what I had witnessed lately at the parties at our house, it didn't seem Mr. Mayer was missing Karl's mom too much.

Still, seeing Karl was anxious about his parents' relationship, I changed the subject, "What did your mother write in her letter to you?"

Karl replied, "She wrote that her brother was sent to the Russian front. It's a dangerous place. If he's shot down, the Russians are notoriously brutal to prisoners of war, particularly those who have been bombing them from the skies."

I nodded sympathetically, trying to comprehend the weight of his concerns.

Karl added, "I hate war. Innocent civilians are targeted. Just like you told me about your cousin Abbas, whose house was bombed in Qazvin by the British. Your cousin is lucky they weren't injured or, even worse, killed. I can't bear the thought of my uncle being a part of something like that, killing innocents."

"You must be worried about his safety; I hope nothing happens to him," I said.

"I am worried," Karl said, then added, "but I don't support this war—especially not one that's all about promoting Nazism and hurting people who have nothing to do with the war. My uncle is a true patriot; he loves Germany and wants to serve, but he wrote to my mother that he is frustrated with politics creeping into everything. He told her many officers felt the same, that enforcing these policies was beneath the Army's dignity."

I told Karl, "Well, I don't know much about Nazis, but I admire the German army's advance through Europe. I am impressed with their military prowess and efficiency. I see it as evidence of German strength and organization, two things my country does not possess; if we did, we wouldn't be occupied."

With a serious look, Karl replied, "Sohrab, my friend, before I came to Iran, I saw the kind of people running things back in Germany."

"What do you mean, Karl? Are you saying the Germans are worse than the British and Russians that invaded my country?"

Karl sighed, choosing his words carefully.

"The situation is complex, Sohrab."

"But why?" I asked. "What harm could come from a German triumph when the British and Russians don't respect our independence? They invade us, occupy us, and humiliate us without a second thought. What's the difference?"

Unaware of the extent of Nazi atrocities, my perspective was limited, and my views were clouded by my anger at seeing Iran humbled by the British and Russians. The Germans were fighting both of them, and considering we were powerless, many Iranians thought as I did, wanting to see the British and Russians humiliated, too. And it looked like the Germans were doing an excellent job of it.

The advent of World War II brought about a wave of fascination that swept through Iran, leading many to lean towards supporting the German cause. Oblivious to the heinous acts committed by the Nazis, they were captivated by a unique aspect of German ideology—the notion that Iranians were considered Aryan people, inheritors of an ancient culture that once birthed the first world empire.

This concept, promoted by the Nazi regime, elevated the Persian heritage to a position of pride and distinction, enticing Iranians to believe in a shared destiny with Germany. Blinded by visions of glory and unaware of the dark depths beneath the Nazi regime's claims, they embraced the pro-German sentiment with admiration.

In 1936, Iranians were classified as "pure-blood Aryans" and thus were excluded from the Nuremberg Laws. I later heard that our king, Reza Shah, informed Hitler that given that Iranian Jews were Iranian, any harm to them would be regarded as a direct offense to the king himself.

It was even rumored that Hitler personally promised that if he defeated the Soviet Union, he would return all of the land taken by Russians from Iran during the nineteenth and twentieth centuries.

At the time, we Iranians didn't know that hidden behind the gloom of war, the true nature of the Nazi regime and its sinister ambitions would soon be revealed.

Krista had also told me a bit about the Nazis, saying she didn't like them and was glad to have left Germany before the war started. She knew friends and relatives who became members of the National Socialist Party not because they were faithful followers but because they wanted to keep their jobs. That's all Krista had said about Nazis. But Karl was about to tell me more.

"You see, there's more to this conflict than meets the eye," he said.

Intrigued, I asked him to explain, and he told me of a terrible event he experienced. "A few months before my father and I came to Iran, I witnessed what people called the 'Night of Broken Glass,'" Karl revealed solemnly. "It was a wave of violent anti-Jewish persecution across Germany." I listened carefully as he described what happened.

"Government officials claimed it was a spontaneous outburst of public sentiment in response to a Jewish gunman's assassination of a German embassy official in Paris," he continued.

"But the truth is, it was a coordinated attack against innocent Jewish people, their businesses, and their places of worship. These Nazis are no good, and no good can come from a German victory in this war."

"Karl, I still don't understand… the Germans targeting Jewish people for one official that was killed? It doesn't make sense," I said.

"No, Sohrab. It goes deeper than that, and it's not just the Jews. The regime in Germany is targeting anyone they consider undesirable or inferior. This includes anyone who disagrees with them. It's a broad and vicious campaign."

Karl's words made me pause. I hadn't fully considered just how widespread the persecution in Germany was. "That's terrible… I know of a Jewish man, Mr. Kahan, who owns a carpet shop in the bazaar," I shared. "My father bought all our home's carpets from him because he told me the man, unlike many in the business, is an honest carpet salesman. I met him once when he and my father had tea at the bazaar. He was very nice and well-respected. No one here would want to harm someone like him."

Karl replied, "Well, there's quite a difference, Sohrab. I'm so glad not to be in Germany now with all that is happening. Here in Iran, I don't see the same level of prejudice as back in Germany. At least the Iranians I've met don't seem to buy into that hate.

"The propaganda and the state's influence back home escalated the savagery. It's a different world there now. I never thought it could happen in Germany, but it has. I fear it could happen anywhere, even right here in Iran, just as quickly. Hate is borderless."

Karl grew increasingly upset as he spoke about the Nazis' actions. I had many questions, but the weight of the conversation seemed to overwhelm him. Suddenly, his gaze shifted to his elegant watch as if seeking refuge in the safety of a lighter, earlier topic.

He offered a strained joke, "You seem taken with my watch. Seeing how much you like it, I'll leave it for you in my will."

The concept of a will was unfamiliar until he elaborated further. His explanation revealed that his death would be how I would inherit his watch. The implication that I desired it so much unsettled me. Sensing the discomfort caused by his ill-timed joke, Karl quickly recovered, telling me that it was a common jest in Germany, and pleaded that I not misunderstand his intent. I gave him a reassuring smile and nodded, hoping to ease the tension and to show him I wasn't taking it to heart.

As we finally arrived at our destination, the modest, arched doorway of the bathhouse entrance invited us into a cool, shadowy interior. As we stepped inside, the clamor of the bustling city faded, replaced by the gentle sound of flowing water and the quiet conversations of men already relaxing in the serene atmosphere. We stripped down, wrapped ourselves in light cotton towels provided by the attendants, and made our way to the main bathing area.

The space was dimly lit, with soft beams of sunlight filtering through small, high-set windows, casting a gentle glow on the mosaic-tiled walls. The warm, humid air clung to our skin as we settled by one of the large marble basins, where water flowed continuously in a steady, soothing stream. In the heart of the public bath, the weight of recent events seemed to dissolve, carried away by the murmuring water.

When we first removed our clothes, I noticed something and wanted to ask Karl. I was thinking of the best way to pose my question. Finally, I gathered the courage and asked, "Why does your... uh, your penis look different?"

Karl was startled, and a brief, uncomfortable silence followed. I regretted asking such a personal question, fearing I might have crossed a line. But Karl understood my curiosity.

"Oh, it's because I'm not circumcised," Karl explained. "In Germany, most boys aren't, but I guess it's the opposite here in Iran, where it seems almost all are circumcised."

Karl chuckled. "One summer, I spent a lot of time with Albert, our housekeeper's son. He was also circumcised."

I asked, "How did you know he was circumcised?"

Karl answered, "Come to think of it, it's a funny story. We often swam at a small lake just a short hike from our house. Whenever we went, there was no one there, but every time, Albert insisted on keeping his underwear on. I knew he was shy, but I always thought it was a strange choice, especially since he had to walk home in wet underwear, looking uncomfortable the whole way."

Karl paused, shaking his head. "Finally, one day, when we went swimming, I noticed Albert hunched over again, trying to hold up his soaked underwear as he exited the lake. It frustrated me that he was so stubborn, so I told him to take them off."

I understood Albert's hesitance as I listened to Karl's story about his friend. I had been shy growing up, especially when it came to being naked. The thought of undressing in front of someone else always made me uncomfortable, and even that day at the bathhouse, I felt a twinge of nervousness about disrobing in Karl's presence.

I asked, "So what did your friend do?"

Karl continued, "Albert mumbled that he wanted to keep them on, but I pressed him, and finally, he admitted that his mother had told him never to take them off."

"Why did his mom tell him that?" I asked.

Karl laughed. "I asked him the same thing—why would his mom care? But he just shrugged, looking embarrassed. After some coaxing, Albert finally peeled off his underwear."

"So that's when you noticed he was circumcised," I stated.

Karl said, "Yes, that was the first time I noticed a difference, that he didn't look like me. And I was just as surprised as when you saw me today."

"It must have been a relief for him not to swim with them on," I said.

Karl replied, "I guess. We just went back in to swim after that. I had forgotten about that day until now."

He paused as if reliving that distant memory. I waited for him to continue, listening closely. Despite the initial awkwardness, the revelation intrigued me, so I couldn't help but press on.

"Did you wonder why he looked different?" I was genuinely curious.

Karl thought for a moment to recall, then said, "I did, but honestly, I forgot until I asked my father sometime later. He wasn't eager to talk about it, only saying, 'Some people do, and some don't.' With a dismissive wave, he added, 'It's as simple as that.'"

I grinned, appreciating Mr. Mayer's straightforward response.

"Have you kept in touch with Albert?" I asked.

Karl's expression turned wistful, his stare drifting as memories flooded back.

"No, not anymore," he said quietly. "My mother told me they suddenly moved to another city where they had relatives, and we lost contact. With the war in Germany now, I hope they're alright."

Chapter 12

"The masses do not necessarily reason. They react. It is upon this reaction that propaganda must be built."

Siegfried Kracauer

Meidan-Sepah (Sepah Square), Tehran, Iran

One afternoon, a few weeks later, Haidar said he was going to Meidan-Sepah to listen to a news broadcast from Radio Berlin's Persian Service and asked if I wanted to come. After my long and uncomfortable conversation with Karl about the war, I was curious about Nazis, so I decided to tag along to hear for myself.

The Sepah Square, a mosaic of old-world charm and wartime urgency, was the stage upon which the drama of distant battlefields unfolded, echoing through speakers positioned high.

As we walked toward the square, Haidar told me that Meidan-Sepah had morphed into a daily stage where people could hear German reports from the war in the company of other Iranians. These gatherings were more than opportunities to catch the news; they were communal experiences for people steeped in anxiety about the events unfolding around them.

When we arrived, it looked more like a sporting event, as people from all walks of life—shopkeepers, mothers, and young workers—clustered around in tight knots. The square felt like the very pulse of the city. There, amidst a sea of concerned faces, stood a radio perched regally on a pedestal, broadcasting German news in Persian.

The Nazis had a radio transmitter in Zeesen, Germany, from where they broadcast programming popular to Iranians under Allied occupation. The Nazis turned the enormous short-wave radio complex there into the world's most potent propaganda machine.

The announcer's voice cut through the crowd's murmur, carrying tales of conflict across continents. The audience hung on every word. Strangers exchanged glances and smiles, reacting to news of German victories as if we were in battle delivering blows to the colonial powers with our own fists.

The crowd's reaction was visceral—cheers would erupt, hands clapped together in applause, resonating through the square like thunder. In those charged moments filled with defiance and shared hope, each German victory seemed to carve a path toward our dreams of autonomy and respect.

"Greetings, esteemed listeners across Iran's vast and noble land!" The voice boomed, clear and enthusiastic.

"This is Radio Zeesen, bringing you the latest news from the battlefields of Europe and beyond! Today, we celebrate another glorious victory for the valiant German forces!"

A collective gasp rippled through the crowd, a wave of anticipation washing over us. Haidar leaned in, a wide grin splitting his face. He was clearly in his element.

"The mighty Wehrmacht has crushed the Soviet siege at Kharkov!" the announcer continued.

"For weeks, the Bolshevik hordes threw themselves against our lines, but German courage and ingenuity have prevailed! Thousands of enemy tanks lie smoldering, their crews scattered like frightened rabbits."

A roar of approval erupted from the multitude. Like the young man beside me, some pumped their fists. A sense of shared triumph surged through the crowd, a feeling I couldn't quite explain. Was it the power of the voice, the promise of a different future, or simply the crowd's energy?

The announcer's voice continued, painting a picture of German dominance. News of Rommel's victories in North Africa followed, further stoking the excitement. An elderly woman beside me, her face etched with worry lines, wiped away a stray tear. Hope flickered in her eyes, a spark I felt in myself.

"The once-invincible British Empire trembles!" the announcer declared.

"From the icy plains of Russia to the arid deserts of Africa, the tide is turning! The forces of freedom, led by the mighty German Reich, are ascendant! Soon, the yoke of colonialism will be broken, and Iran, like all nations, will take its rightful place as a free and independent state!"

The radio announcer's voice ignited a thunderous roar of approval. I glanced at Haidar, his face a mixture of excitement and a hint of something else, perhaps apprehension. The crowd surged with raw energy, a cocktail of emotions swirling around us.

As the broadcast ended, the radio fell silent. The electricity in the air remained a tangible force connecting all of us at that moment. The news from Radio Zeesen painted a picture of a world teetering on the brink. In this world, the Germans were on the cusp of victory, where Iran could finally be freed from British and Russian dominance.

Haidar had told me about an evening in the poorer quarters of Tehran, where a crowd in a dingy cinema erupted in cheers for Hitler during a British war film, jeering and celebrating at all the wrong moments. It was a clear example of the effectiveness of these broadcasts.

An overly excited man beside me leaned in close, his voice barely audible over the clamor.

"You know," he began, his voice laced with intrigue, "I heard something incredible on the broadcast last week. They said Hitler converted to Shiism—can you believe it? Some even call him the last Imam who has come to save us from the shackles of the British and communists."

I couldn't help but chuckle at the absurdity of Hitler becoming a Muslim. This man's outlandish belief reflected the strange desperation and fantasy these broadcasts stirred within Iranians.

This potent mix made even the most improbable rumors seem like gospel. Berlin recognized that the racially charged antisemitism prevalent in Germany wouldn't find fertile ground in Iran, as the concept of race held little significance for most Iranians. Therefore, Germany placed all its emphasis on religious motifs in these broadcasts.

But amid the cheers and the jubilation, a question remained unanswered: Was this optimism, or were we clinging to a carefully crafted illusion?

It was an unsettling spectacle; I wondered if the masses were swayed not by truth but by the manipulative prowess of distant broadcasters. It later became apparent to me that these orchestrators of sentiment were no different from the mullahs who preyed on the ignorance of our people—both exploiting beliefs and superstitions for their own ends.

The holy men, draped in the sanctity of faith, wielded tales of divine sanction as skillfully as the propagandists wielded their broadcasts, feeding the fantasies that so quickly ensnared the desperate.

Yet, through the zeal and misplaced cheers, something nagged at me. If the fervent waves of propaganda could weaken our occupiers, then maybe harnessing the ignorance of the masses was acceptable.

It was a troubling concession, wrestling with the morality of using deceit as a tool for liberation. The battle for our nation's soul was as much within us as it was against our invaders.

After a few months, the British, troubled by this fervor, pressured Iranian authorities to remove all radios from public places to stem the tide of German influence. However, it was a lost cause, considering that listening in private houses was still widely practiced. Many people who listened were convinced that the Axis powers would win the war, with Hitler enjoying great personal popularity.

But later, in an ironic twist, the public radios were swiftly restored—again at British insistence—when it was realized that without them, no one could tune into the broadcasts from London either. The radios returned, and with them, the daily ritual of gathering, listening, and, for some, dreaming of a different outcome to the war.

"This constant lie is not intended to make the people believe a lie, but to make no one believe anything anymore. A people that can no longer distinguish between truth and falsehood, cannot distinguish between right and wrong. And such a people, which considers itself deprived of its power, to think and to judge, is also, without knowing or wanting, completely subject to the law of lying. With such a people, you can do whatever you want."

Hannah Arendt

CHAPTER 13

"The best weapon against an enemy is another enemy."
Friedrich Nietzsche

With the Russian occupation of northern Iran, our father's import-export trade was halted. Arash, who had always lived a life of financial ease, now found himself in an unfamiliar and troubling situation.

He was accustomed to a luxurious lifestyle where indulgence was the norm. But now, that same lifestyle had become a heavy burden. The household's expensive upkeep added to the pressure. With financial concerns looming large, Arash found the grim reality of his situation unsettling. He needed to find a way to sustain the family, unsure how long the occupation would continue.

Despite his lack of business experience, Arash felt a strong urge to take action. He saw a potential opportunity to export cotton to Russia, utilizing the invader-occupiers' merchant vessels at the port of Bandar Pahlavi outside of Rasht for transport across the Caspian Sea.

Arash's plan was fraught with risk during wartime. He was stepping far out of his comfort zone, preparing to negotiate with the Russians. The uncertainty of the outcome and the inherent dangers of dealing with foreign occupiers heightened his anxiety.

Arash decided to go big to make it work but knew he didn't have enough money and needed to borrow a substantial sum for the venture. He planned to ship enough goods to secure their future with the profits, believing this may be his only chance to pull it off.

He met with his father's business partners in the bazaar, offering them an opportunity to invest in his bold plan. Arash collected a significant amount with nothing but a handshake, relying on our family's well-known and respected name.

🐈🐈🐈

We had heard that Qazvin, where my cousin Abbas lived, had suffered even more damage than Tehran during the bombings, though the Allies had hit both cities. Karl, always adventurous, was eager to see the effects of the war up close.

I was frightened by the idea and was surprised by Karl's enthusiasm. But his excitement was infectious, and before long, he convinced me to put my fear aside and ask Arash about the trip. Karl promised to speak with his father as well. At first, they were hesitant, but finally, both Arash and Mr. Mayer permitted us to go.

My brother agreed to drop us off at Abbas's trucking company in Qazvin on his way to Rasht, where he planned to secure a cotton deal. Since Arash wouldn't be returning to Tehran with us, he insisted that Haidar accompany us, knowing the dangers we might face. Haidar's presence would provide the protection we needed.

The journey to Qazvin was perilous. The road was dotted with numerous checkpoints, petrol was scarce, and some of the road surfaces were damaged by tanks and bombs, making every mile a calculated risk.

When we left Tehran for Qazvin, Arash warned Karl, who spoke English, to act as if he were British, knowing the Russians would be suspicious of a German. The last thing we needed was additional scrutiny at a checkpoint.

Once we arrived in Qazvin, the sight of tanks and armored vehicles patrolling the streets served as an ominous reminder of the ongoing conflict. You could feel the tension as their looming presence cast a shadow of fear and uncertainty over the city.

Arash dropped us off and continued to Rasht. My cousin walked us back toward his house as we explored the city's dusty streets. The signs of Allied occupation were evident everywhere. The people were subdued, and I couldn't help but feel anger at the sight of the invaders in my beloved Iran, as if our sovereignty meant nothing to them.

Some buildings stood in ruins, with shattered walls and caved-in roofs. The vibrant sounds of merchants and buyers haggling were replaced by distant gunshots and the somber silence of fear. Once a prosperous hub of culture and commerce, Qazvin streets were now desolate.

Staring at the foreign soldiers patrolling the streets, Haidar became upset and mumbled curses. With an expression of sorrow and fury, Abbas led us through a maze of broken alleyways.

"Look around," he said, gesturing to a pile of rubble that was once a vibrant home, "This is the gift the Allies have brought us. It's one thing to wage war but quite another to rob a nation of its soul."

Haidar, usually reserved and composed, struggled to hide his despair.

"These were homes, Abbas? It looks more like a graveyard. These stones held stories, laughter, and dreams. Now, what do they hold? May God damn these occupiers!"

"I know, Haidar," Abbas replied, his voice strained. "But what eats at me even more is that they didn't stop at our homes. They are taking our food. The grain meant to sustain our families is now being shipped off to feed soldiers in Russia fighting the Germans."

I looked over at Haidar, whose hands were clenched into fists. "Taking food out of our mouths to feed our invaders? This is an injustice," Haidar declared.

"I don't know how, but I swear by my ancestors I will find a way to help our people. They shouldn't be starving for a war they never wanted."

As we continued our walk, Abbas added, with a heavy sigh, "To add to the hardship, they've taken over my company's trucks and drivers to transport these supplies up north. I despise it, but I have no choice. The income they offer is the only way to rebuild… to feed my own family."

Haidar told him, "I understand, Abbas. We must make sacrifices and choices we never imagined in these trying times. But remember, we are Iranians. We've faced invaders in the past—Greeks, Romans, Arabs, and Mongols—and we have emerged stronger. *Inshallah* (God-willing), we will again."

Caught up in his feelings and the need to express my bitterness, I turned to Karl and said, "Seeing this makes me want Germany to win the war!"

Karl replied, "Don't wish for what you don't know."

I asked, "What is it that I don't know?"

He said, "We've talked about this and don't seem to agree. Let's leave it; I don't want to argue."

I pointed to a bomb-damaged house on the side of the street. "There is nothing to argue about. My country was neutral in Europe's war. My father warned me that the Russians and the British would invade and occupy our land if they couldn't manipulate our rulers. No one would expect us to fight and defend ourselves against two major European powers for more than a few days. The way I see it, the Germans are fighting both of my enemies at the same time. The enemy of my enemy is my friend."

Karl nodded to let me know he understood, "But war makes a strange bedfellow out of an enemy's enemy. You may unknowingly be praying for a different occupier if Germany wins, that's all."

What Karl said was insightful, but at that moment, I was too angry to see the truth in it.

As we arrived at my cousin's house, the ravages of war were unmistakably clear. A bomb had torn through part of his home, showing no mercy despite Abbas's desperate attempt to protect it. He had draped red parchments on his roof, believing, as many in Rasht had, that this would signal allegiance to the Soviets and spare him from their air raids. In Rasht, red, the color of communism and the Soviet flag, symbolized loyalty that seemingly deterred Russian bombs.

Abbas had assumed that Qazvin would face the same threat from the Russian Air Force. However, he soon realized his grave error—red was no shield against the British Royal Air Force, whose bombs had rained down instead.

After exploring his house's damaged surroundings, we needed to find a place to eat. Abbas suggested we visit a neighborhood untouched by the bombs. In contrast to the devastation we had just witnessed, this area seemed blissfully unaware of the nearby war. Abbas escorted us into a restaurant he frequented at the edge of town.

Before we entered the eatery, I noticed a group of rough-looking men heading our way. They had a certain air about them—tough, hardened. I felt a knot of unease form in my stomach. Their swagger, the way they moved together, made me nervous. I was relieved when we stepped inside the restaurant, the warm smell of food greeting us, and I thought we had left them behind. But once we sat down, I spotted them again—they'd followed us in and taken a table nearby.

I leaned toward Abbas and muttered, "Those guys look... intimidating."

Abbas chuckled softly and shook his head. "No worries," he said, waving a hand dismissively. "They're just *lutis*. They won't bother us."

Lutigari, which embodies the principles of chivalry, has deep roots in Iranian urban culture. A luti is a formidable figure within the neighborhood, sort of a local champion who upholds justice in the community. The luti's role is derived from his physical strength, not driven by aspirations for leadership or personal gain. Recognized for his honesty and physical prowess, a luti will frequently serve as the guardian of the community, patrolling the streets and providing aid to those in need. He inspires respect and fear due to his occasional adoption of thuggish tactics to intimidate adversaries into submission.

Abbas sensed my unease and asked, "Have you ever had alcohol before?"

I nodded. "Well, once. Krista gave me some wine at dinner."

Abbas smirked. "Wine? No, no. I mean a real drink."

I raised an eyebrow. "A real drink?"

"*Arak*," (a strong alcoholic beverage) Abbas clarified, a grin spreading across his face. "Let's order a bottle for the table."

Before I knew it, Abbas had already waved down the waiter and ordered a bottle of arak. When it arrived, he poured some for all of us. He filled our glasses with much more than I had anticipated. I hesitated but took a sip, the fiery liquid warming me from the inside out.

Within minutes, I could feel my head growing warmer, a strange but pleasant sensation spreading through me. The sounds of the restaurant—the clinking of glasses, the chatter, and the faint hum of conversation—began to blend, creating a soft, rhythmic background. The warmth of the drink made everything seem more relaxed, and I found myself smiling, enjoying the moment.

For a while, I forgot about the tough guys sitting nearby, the tension that had gripped me earlier melting away. Abbas laughed, telling stories about our family, and I listened, feeling more at ease with every sip.

Out of the corner of my eye, I saw the lutis ordering their own bottles, and soon, their boisterous laughter filled the air, startling the other patrons. Some uncomfortable customers hastily left, disturbed by the growing commotion.

Sensing the rising tension, I turned to Abbas and proposed that we leave. But he remained unperturbed, calmly taking a drag from his cigarette. He grinned and said, "Don't worry, they're harmless."

Moments later, chaos erupted at the lutis' table. The sound of breaking arak bottles mixed with heated shouts drew the attention of everyone left in the establishment. Two men stood up, engaged in a fierce argument. Abbas and Haidar were unfazed, as if they had seen this scene before, while Karl and I exchanged anxious glances.

I asked Abbas if now was the time to go. Once again, he smiled and said, "Why should we leave now? We'll miss the show."

Abbas knew the brawlers. He told us Kazem Kaghi, nicknamed Kazem *kharchang* (Kazem the crab), was the guy with his coat wrapped around his forearm for protection and brandishing a switchblade. He also knew the man's opponent, a much larger and more robust fellow named Morteza *gorbeh* (Morteza the cat), who met the challenge head-on.

Chairs and tables crashed as Kazem lunged at his opponent, their disagreement evolving into a dangerous knife fight dance atop the bar counter. One of Kazem's charges proved effective as he slashed the cheek of Morteza, and blood flowed all over the bar.

The proprietor had already called the police, and soon, officers arrived to quell the brawl. Kazem and Morteza were promptly arrested. Curiosity overwhelmed us as we watched the events unfold, unsure of what had transpired.

The police restrained the combatants and questioned them about the cause of the fight. Kazem, breathless and filled with rage, shouted, "This son of a bitch went with my woman!"

Morteza, seemingly unaffected, sneered, "But she's a whore. It's her job."

Kazem reacted instantly to his comment and lunged at the man. Restrained by the officers, one admonished him, "Kazem, what's your problem? You were just released from jail a few days ago. Do you want to go back again?"

Kazem countered, his face contorted with anger, "I pray for jail. Prison would be my savior!"

Morteza the cat said he did not want to press charges, so the police forced the men to shake and make up, which they did reluctantly and for show.

Abbas told us, "These street tough guys adhere to their code of conduct. According to their rules, no luti is supposed to be involved with another man's woman, even if she is a prostitute. It's considered dishonorable in their world."

Abbas paused momentarily, unable to explain Kazem's curious desire for jail. "That part's a mystery to me; I don't know what Kazem meant," he added.

The following day, before we returned to Tehran, news spread like wildfire through the city. We were shocked to learn that Kazem visited his woman, and in a rage, he stabbed her multiple times, leaving her to die in the doorway of her home. The reason behind Kazem's earlier prayer for jail became clear—this time, there would be no refuge in a prison cell, only the judgment of the hangman's noose.

"But why did he kill her if he loved her?" A confused Karl asked upon hearing the news.

Abbas, his eyes heavy with sorrow, shook his head slowly.

"Because he loved his honor more," he said.

The words hung heavy in the air, their implications sinking like a lead weight into Karl's heart. This revelation prompted him to ask Abbas, "So, a man will be ready to die for this honor?"

With a weary sigh, Abbas nodded, "A man, foolishly believing he is protecting his honor, will kill for it and even be ready to die for it, as we have just unfortunately witnessed," he explained.

Karl seemed visibly moved, and as if talking to himself, he mumbled, "It sounds romantic... he loved her so much...."

Karl's voice trailed off, his mind grappling to understand the perverted reason that drove Kazem to commit such a despicable act.

Abbas heard Karl and responded with a severe warning: "Don't romanticize it! My father used to say if you embark on a journey of revenge, dig two graves first. Why do you foreigners always find something exotic about things like this? Don't be foolish. What he did is just the tragic consequence of misplaced values!"

I asked myself, *What honor drives a man to pierce the heart of someone he loves?* The concept of honor seemed twisted, an elusive ideal that leads men down dark paths they never wish to tread. And just as a distorted sense of honor drove Kazem to commit his savage act, the invading Russian and British soldiers likely believed that their ruthless actions were justified by their own warped ideals of honor and duty.

The notion of honor felt like a hollow excuse, a mask concealing the raw ambition of power and control, distorted into something unrecognizable, a weapon wielded by those who sought to dominate and oppress. Yet, all I saw was destruction, nothing honorable.

On our return trip to Tehran, bound by the shared horror of what we had seen, the lines between honor, love, and vengeance blurred in our minds. I turned to Karl, unable to hold back, "I wish you hadn't convinced us to go," I murmured. As the familiar streets of our neighborhood came into view, I felt relieved. However, even in the safety of our home, the shadows of Qazvin lingered, refusing to fade.

CHAPTER 14

"Don't grieve. Anything you lose comes round in another form."

Rumi

Aleksandr Khadeyev was a seasoned Russian political commissar responsible for ensuring the military's loyalty to the Communist Party and directing the political education of the troops. His posting in the Caspian basin was strategic: to oversee the vital Allied supply routes and as guardian of the Soviet Union's southern frontier.

Commissar Khadeyev was born in the foothills of the Ural Mountains in a small industrial town that flourished amid the growth of the Russian Empire's steel industry. The son of a factory worker and a nurse, he grew up with a strong work ethic and a belief in the promise of a better future for the working class. Like his father, Khadeyev was expected to work in the town's burgeoning steel factory.

His early years were marked by the turbulent upheavals of Russia's political landscape. As a young man, he witnessed the fall of the Tsarist regime and the ensuing chaos that gripped his nation. The civil war that followed the October Revolution of 1917 swept Khadeyev into the tide of history.

As the old empires of Europe crumbled and the Bolsheviks seized the reins of power, he joined the Red

Army, driven by a passionate hatred for the old regime and a fervent belief in the Bolshevik cause. During these formative years, Khadeyev's resolve was hardened by the unforgiving realities of war. He quickly rose through the ranks, and his strategic acumen and unyielding dedication to the cause earned him the respect of his comrades and superiors.

But the scars of war were not just physical for him; they were etched into his soul. He saw firsthand the devastation wrought by foreign intervention and the White armies supported by Western powers, including the dreaded fascist elements that would soon plague Europe.

His distaste for the Germans traced back to the Great War, when tales of the Eastern Front's horrors filtered back to his hometown, stories of merciless advances and brutal occupations that painted the Germans as ruthless aggressors devoid of honor or humanity.

These narratives, which shaped his early nationalist education, were further reinforced by the Soviet Union's post-war experiences, including the punitive terms of the Treaty of Brest-Litovsk, which imposed severe penalties and territorial losses on Russia.

The treaty was unpopular in Russia because it gave away too much land. As a result, Russia lost almost a third of its rich agricultural production. For Khadeyev, these were not only diplomatic grievances but an assault upon the very essence of his homeland, evidence of German ambition and oppression.

The rise of fascism in Germany, with its ideologies of racial superiority and expansionist dreams, only served to deepen Khadeyev's contempt. He saw in it a continuation of the same imperialistic hunger that had led to the suffering of his people decades earlier.

He hated fascists. The Russian Commissar often dismissed the Germans as "the Huns." In his view, they were the inheritors of the Hunnish legacy, barbarians eager to spread their doctrine of domination and oppression across the globe.

The Commissar was an imposing figure, the contours of his face etched by the passage of time and the burdens of command. His complexion was weathered, not unlike the rugged landscapes of his homeland.

Khadeyev's probing stare could unravel the most carefully guarded secrets. His eyes flashed with the intensity of a man who had seen many things and could decipher the motives of friends and foes alike with incisive clarity.

His uniform was always pristine, the cloth crisp, and the medals and insignia polished to a gleam. It reflected his unwavering discipline and symbolized his pride in representing his office and country.

As Khadeyev looked out over Rasht, he reflected on his recent successes. In his short tenure, he consolidated his authority and neutralized potential threats by orchestrating high-profile arrests and intense interrogations.

Khadeyev's message was clear: defiance would not be tolerated. His methods were ruthless, but they had achieved the desired result, and the locals now understood that their city was under his firm control.

🐈 🐈 🐈

Arash embarked on the 200-kilometer drive north from Qazvin to Rasht, where potential dangers lurked ahead. Each twist and turn, along with every checkpoint, intensified the suspense and uncertainty of the journey.

As he drove, he was constantly on edge, scanning the horizon for any signs of trouble. The mountainous terrain, with its countless hiding spots, was perfect for ambushes. He knew bandits could be waiting, ready to prey on lone travelers like himself.

He had brought an emergency canister of petrol from Qazvin to ensure he wouldn't run out of fuel. But the situation's unpredictability still worried him. Despite his precautions, there was no telling what dangers might lie ahead.

Arash's mind raced with thoughts of what might await him in Rasht, a city now under Russian control. He had heard stories of the strict curfews, Russian troops patrolling the streets, and the general unease among the local population.

The prospect of negotiating with the Russians in such an environment was intimidating. Arash didn't know what to expect—whether he would be met with suspicion, hostility, or indifference. The lack of reliable information about Rasht's current state only added to his anxiety.

Arash knew his family depended on the success of his mission, and he steeled himself for the challenges ahead, hoping that his determination and quick thinking would see him through safely.

Once he arrived in Rasht, Arash realized how difficult it was to secure an appointment with the local Russian commander, Khadeyev. Despite his persistent efforts, he waited for days, trapped in his hotel with no clear timeline.

The bureaucratic hurdles were overwhelming, and every inquiry led to another dead end. The local officials were unhelpful, often ignoring his requests or redirecting him to other departments.

After a week of fruitless waiting and mounting frustration, Arash was approached by a local who discreetly suggested that a bribe might expedite the process. Desperate and running out of time, Arash reluctantly followed the advice. He secretly offered money to a clerk who had previously ignored him.

The next day, he received a message: his appointment with Khadeyev was scheduled. Arash was finally granted a brief half-hour meeting with the Russian Commissar. With only a small window of time to present his case, he prepared meticulously, knowing that this was his one chance to secure the deal his family desperately needed.

Arash was invited into a room adorned with a giant portrait of Stalin, his stern gaze seemingly judging every word spoken within those walls. The room was dimly lit, with the heavy drapes pulled tight against the afternoon sun. Khadeyev, his stare penetrating, lounged behind his imposing desk, with his fingers idly drumming on its surface.

Arash's heart sank as he realized the gravity of the task ahead. The Commissar seemed disinterested as Arash spoke, barely glancing at the documents he had painstakingly prepared. It appeared as though the meeting would be a failure.

However, while Arash eagerly explained the potential benefits of their cotton trade deal, he casually mentioned the significant profits and mutual benefits that could arise from future collaborations.

At the mention of profits, the Commissar's demeanor began to shift. This man loved to make money, and the idea of a lucrative deal piqued his interest. Khadeyev's facade cracked, revealing a calculating mind behind those cold eyes. He leaned forward, suddenly more engaged, and asked questions about the logistics and potential earnings.

Seizing the opportunity, Arash elaborated on how their partnership could provide a steady and lucrative supply line. He painted a vivid picture of the wealth that could come from such a deal, tapping into the Russian's evident ambition and greed. Arash also highlighted the strategic importance of cotton, which would be used to clothe Soviet soldiers fighting the Germans. This practical advantage added another layer of appeal for Khadeyev, aligning the deal with the broader war effort and boosting his standing with his superiors.

The room grew warmer as the conversation flowed, the initial frostiness thawing in the face of shared interests. Khadeyev's eyes glittered with the prospect of personal gain, and a slow smile spread across his face.

Here was a man who relished the power and prestige that came with wealth, and Arash's proposal promised both. Convinced that the opportunity would enhance his reputation, Khadeyev agreed to Arash's proposal, granting him the necessary permissions to proceed.

The Russian leaned back and nodded. "Very well, Mr. Ahangar," he said, his tone now markedly warmer.

"Now that I have agreed to your venture, you must make sure the shipments are on time and of the highest quality. Don't forget, I am also taking a big risk here. Any mishap or delay will have serious consequences."

Arash found himself in a difficult position, forced to agree to the Commissar's terms even though he would take on most of the risk. Despite this, the relief of finally securing a deal filled him with optimism. He trusted his plan and was confident in his ability to execute it.

Determined to leave no room for error, Arash remained in Rasht to oversee every detail, from sourcing the cotton to ensuring its safe loading onto the ships destined for Khadeyev's contacts back in Russia. His presence on the ground would allow him to address any unforeseen complications swiftly and further solidify the newfound trust with the Russian commander.

Immediately after meeting with the Commissar, Arash sprang into action. A key aspect of his plan hinged on his knowledge of the high-quality cotton cultivated in the Caspian region—a product renowned for its superior texture and durability. Furthermore, Iranian cotton's affordability compared to Egyptian alternatives, which would incur additional shipping costs, presented a lucrative opportunity.

The venture's success hinged on securing a sufficient supply from the numerous small-scale cotton producers in the region. After weeks of relentless effort—traveling between villages, negotiating with local merchants, and coordinating logistics—Arash finally procured enough cotton to fulfill the order. He promptly arranged its transportation to the port and oversaw its loading onto a Soviet merchant ship bound for Russia.

After so much time and hard work, Arash felt a tremendous sense of relief. He returned to his hotel, confident the cargo would take several days to reach its destination. As he rested in his room, he couldn't help but wish his father were alive to witness this achievement. Securing such a bold deal with the Russians was a testament to his business acumen, and he knew his father would have been proud of him.

Exhausted from his endeavors, he didn't notice the growing storm outside his window as he fell asleep. The sky darkened threateningly, and the sea began to roar.

That evening, a full-blown storm on the Caspian battered the Russian ship. Towering waves crashed against the vessel as the captain and crew fought bravely to keep it afloat, adjusting their course, desperate to stabilize the boat. The wind howled, shaking the metal structure, and the rain lashed down in torrents, reducing visibility to almost nothing.

Despite their valiant efforts, it was useless. The storm was too powerful, and the ship began to list dangerously as the water poured in. The captain, a seasoned seafarer with years of experience, knew they were in danger of sinking. The unceasing battering of the waves was too much for the ship to endure.

In a desperate bid to save the vessel and its crew, the captain made a heartbreaking decision. He ordered the jettison of Arash's precious cotton. The crew worked frantically, heaving the bales overboard into the churning waters. As the cotton disappeared into the stormy sea, so went Arash's dreams of a quick fortune.

🐈🐈🐈

On the day the cargo should have reached its destination in Russia, Arash anxiously entered Khadeyev's office, his heart pounding with hope.

With a serious expression, the Russian looked up from his paperwork and said, "Mr. Ahangar, please have a seat," gesturing towards the chair before him. Arash sat down, fidgeting with his hat nervously.

"Commissar, I trust you bring me good news. What has happened to the cargo? Did the ship make it safely to Russia?"

The Commissar paused, narrowing his gaze as he measured the weight of his words.

"Mr. Ahangar, I regret that disaster struck our ship on the Caspian Sea. A violent storm raged, endangering the vessel. Desperate to save the crew and the ship, the captain decided to dump the cotton cargo overboard."

Arash's face turned white with shock, his mind struggling to comprehend the gravity of the situation.

"What…All of it? Our entire cargo, gone?"

Khadeyev nodded solemnly. "Yes, I'm afraid so. It is a terrible loss. I've been told they did everything possible, but sometimes nature's fury cannot be tamed."

Arash couldn't believe it, especially the Commissar's matter-of-fact retelling of how the bales were thrown overboard into the stormy abyss. Hearing the gut-wrenching news, Arash clenched his fists in frustration; financially and emotionally, he was devastated.

He had pinned his future on this deal, and now, with the cargo lost to the storm, he didn't know how to pay back the investors. The storm claimed more than the cotton; it crushed his spirit as Arash wondered how to rebuild from the wreckage.

"What am I to do now, Commissar? The investors in Tehran expect their money back, but I have nothing to offer them without the profits from this venture."

The Russian leaned back in his chair and took a drag of his cigarette with a contemplative look.

"Mr. Ahangar, I have no concern for who you owe in Tehran. I am only concerned with my loss. Please understand that I cannot let you leave Rasht without settling your debts here. You owe us, including the cost of hiring the ship, the captain, and the crew, even if the cargo was lost."

Arash was stunned, his breath quickening as his voice trembled.

"But I have nothing left. I have no means to repay you!"

Even though Khadeyev's voice softened slightly, he dismissed Arash's plea.

"In any case, you shall remain here in Rasht as our guest until you can find a way to repay your debts. I will not burden your family in Tehran for now, but you must work diligently to rectify the situation."

Remaining in Rasht offered temporary respite from his creditors in Tehran, buying Arash time to formulate a plan. But it also meant he would be indefinitely separated from Krista and his family.

Arash nodded, knowing he was at the mercy of whatever the Commissar wanted to do. Going through the motions, he gave the Russian a firm handshake, left his office, and returned to his hotel under guard. His mind raced with thoughts of his family, the debts he owed, and the uncertain future that lay ahead.

🐱🐱🐱

Meanwhile, in Tehran, we were optimistic about the outcome of Arash's plan and waited impatiently for news about the deal. When Arash returned from Germany after my father's passing, he brought hope to our family. We believed he had the determination and drive to resurrect our family's faltering business.

When he finally called Krista, he urged her to stall the bazaari investors while not explaining the circumstances that kept him in Rasht. We wondered if it was going so well that he had to extend his stay in the north to attend to even more business. Krista excitedly told me that she wanted to renovate and redecorate the mansion and was eager to do so with the profits from Arash's deal.

As the days passed, we waited for further updates from him. During this time, Krista and I spent many afternoons lounging by the ornamental pool and talking in the courtyard, where the sun cast long shadows and pomegranate blossoms painted the earth with hints of crimson.

One such afternoon, the conversation steered towards Krista's life with Arash in Munich. She told me tales of their courtship as her face glowed with the ghost of past joy, recalling the quaint cafes and their blossoming love.

"You know, Arash was my first real boyfriend. I wasn't seriously involved with anyone before him. I remember how he made me feel like the most cherished being on earth," Krista murmured nostalgically.

She painted a tale of love, as her cheerful façade slightly lifted, revealing a deep longing—something she wanted to share. I nodded, urging her to continue, curious about Krista's past with Arash in Germany.

"I wasn't ready to marry. I wanted to finish my studies. But your brother was so persistent," she admitted with a small, wistful smile.

"He was always trying to convince me, promising a better life. You see, things in Germany were tough, getting worse economically. Arash painted this picture of Iran—a life of wealth, with servants and gardeners, something that sounded alluring. He told me it would only be for a short while but that he has plans for us to go back and live in Germany when things settle down."

I could see the conflict in her expression, the struggle between yesterday's dreams and today's realities.

"My parents were initially against it," Krista confided.

"The idea of their daughter marrying a foreigner and moving to Iran was unthinkable. But they also were experiencing the same hardships and eventually understood, even accepted my decision."

Krista continued, her voice tinged with melancholy.

"I had heard, you know, that love grows over time," Krista said, tracing a pattern on the shawl draped over her knees. "They say that when children are born into a marriage, they cement the relationship, bringing the couple closer."

She looked into the distance and said, "I believed our love would blossom, especially if we were blessed with children."

Krista paused and then mused aloud, "But now," she added, "I find myself questioning that belief. I... I'm just not sure anymore."

Krista took a deep breath, "In the streets of Munich, I watched mothers with their children, thinking someday it would be the same for me. But time has passed, and our home remains silent," she sighed.

Krista's voice trembled as she navigated through her concealed anguish.

"The heavens have yet to grace us with such joy... and sometimes I wonder,... I wonder if there's something amiss with us."

I didn't know what she meant and worried they were having problems.

I asked, "What do you mean amiss?"

Krista said, "Maybe we won't ever have children."

Her voice trembled under the weight of the revelation. A sorrow-filled sigh escaped her lips as she attempted to come to terms with the reality of what she shared—words that must have been swirling around in her mind for a while.

The silence that followed was uncomfortably long. So, to fill the vacuum, I asked, "What does Arash say?"

She hesitated, "Arash says we should be patient, and God has a plan for us. But sometimes I wonder... What if God's plan for us is not to have children? I'm beginning to think that He may have closed that door."

Chapter 15

*"I am not afraid of storms,
for I am learning how to sail my ship."*

Louisa May Alcott

Krista moved forward with her plans to redecorate the mansion by selling off items and making room for the new furniture. It was reassuring to know that Arash's business deal was going well, as she told me she would fund the redecoration with those profits.

One day, she asked me, "Where did you buy the magnificent carpets in our living and dining rooms?"

"From Mr. Kahan," I replied. "He's an old friend of my father from the bazaar."

Her face lit up. "Would you join me in going to Mr. Kahan's shop? I don't want to go alone."

"Of course," I said. "If you don't mind, I'll let Karl know he's welcome to come, too."

Krista agreed, and when I met with Karl that afternoon, I reminded him about my father's friend who owns a carpet shop.

"Krista and I are going tomorrow; join us if you want. You'll be impressed with how they pile hundreds of carpets on each other and how the workers can find the exact color and pattern you want, like a needle in a haystack."

Karl got excited and eagerly agreed to tag along.

The following day, we set out for the bazaar, a bustling maze of sights and sounds. The air was filled with the intoxicating aroma of spices as vendors' cries weaved through the bustling marketplace, each vying for the attention of passersby. The atmosphere was lively, filled with the clamor of haggling buyers and sellers.

Mr. Kahan's shop was a modest but inviting establishment with carpets of all sizes and colors stacked in towering piles. The Jewish shopkeeper, an older man of short stature with a kind face, greeted us warmly. His store was a kaleidoscope of rich textiles, each telling its own story.

"Good morning, Mr. Kahan," I said, respectfully bowing my head with my hand on my chest.

"I am Sohrab Ahangar. I don't know if you remember me, Mohammad's son?"

"Good morning, of course, welcome," he responded, his voice filled with the warmth of long-standing familiarity with my family.

"God bless your father's soul; he was a good man. How can I assist you today?"

Krista and I exchanged pleasantries with him. Karl greeted Mr. Kahan with a single *"Salam."*

Upon hearing Karl's accent, a hint of curiosity crossed Mr. Kahan's face. *"Shoma mal-e kojaee?"* (Where are you from?) he asked Karl.

"Aleman" (Germany)," he replied.

Mr. Kahan shook his head with sadness, *"Alan Aleman oza aslan khoob nist"* (It's not good in Germany; what's happening there now).

Karl's hands twitched slightly, a nervous habit he had when anxious. He nodded, responding in his best attempt at Persian, *"Baleh agha, khaili bad-e."* (You are correct, sir. It's terrible).

Mr. Kahan sighed, "Thank God for the great King Cyrus, who brought my Jewish ancestors to this land thousands of years ago. We have lived and died here for generations. Even Esther and Mordechai, our revered figures, are buried here. We have no such worries; Iran is our home."

His discomfort was evident as he spoke, "But let's not dwell on such matters. How can I help you today?"

Krista seized the moment, "I'm considering selling the two rugs my late father-in-law bought from you. Do you remember them?"

I turned to Krista, curiosity gnawing at me, "Why are you selling the rugs?"

She hesitated, her eyes darting away.

"I told you, Sohrab, for redecoration," she said, seemingly irritated by my question.

I thought we had come to Mr. Kahan's shop to buy carpets, not sell them; I felt there was more to the story, something she had yet to share.

Then Krista immediately returned to the business and said, "So what do you think, Mr. Kahan?"

Mr. Kahan, recalling the carpets, agreed. "Ah yes, those are beautiful pieces. I will send my clerk to come check them out. I would gladly buy them back."

🐈 🐈 🐈

Days later, Haidar came and told me, "Sohrab Khan, I am leaving to work for your cousin Abbas in Qazvin as a driver for his trucking company transporting supplies for the Allies."

Surprised about his plan, I asked, "But why so suddenly, Haidar?"

He replied, "I hung on as long as possible, but I need to send money back to my family in the village. They are depending on me."

Haidar's comment confused me, so I questioned, "Aren't we paying you enough that you have to get another job?"

He said, "Sohrab Khan, I haven't been paid in months. It seems your family is having financial trouble. Haven't you noticed Krista Khanoom has been selling the furniture to make ends meet?"

It was then I realized how naive I was. Things were happening around me, and I had been looking the other way.

I asked Krista if what Haidar told me was true. She hesitated before admitting we were having trouble. She shared that the bazaari investors were initially amicable and patient but had grown increasingly aggressive in their demands as time passed.

Krista told me Arash had written to her and explained his grave situation. In his letter, he tried to reassure her, urging her not to worry and promising he would find a solution. But Krista decided to do whatever she could to pay off the most belligerent investors and procure some funds to run the household. She wasn't eager to tell me more, as if she were hiding something from me.

But I didn't let it go. I wanted to know how Krista had been managing things, and I was curious if there was anything else she hadn't told me.

She tried to change the subject, but I pressed, "So how did you handle the bazaari investors then?"

Finally, Krista relented and told me what had happened.

"When Arash's business venture went awry, we wanted to keep it a secret as long as possible, but now all our money is gone. The investors lost their patience and wanted their money back with interest. I didn't know what to do or where to turn, so I went to the bazaar to meet with Haj Mirza Ali Khan, to whom we owed the most. I had never met him, given that Arash negotiated with the investors.

"When I first arrived at his office, he was cordial. He sat behind his cluttered desk, and we shared some small talk. But after a few minutes, he got up, pulled a chair, and sat uncomfortably close to me.

"I tried to move my chair back and told him I was there to discuss the money we owed him. I said we were in a difficult situation with the Russians keeping Arash in Rasht and asked if we could do anything to settle our debt.

"Then he leaned in with his large, sweaty hand, covered in coarse black hair, which he laid on my knee. His firm grip, with the carnelian ring he wore, dug into my skin. I realized I had made a terrible mistake going alone."

Krista paused briefly, but her face couldn't hide her disgust at the memory of the man's affront. I was dumbfounded that an associate of my father had treated my sweet sister-in-law that way. Her story shocked me to my core.

Krista swallowed hard, a lump formed in her throat, and then she began to cry. I waited for her to collect herself, as she seemed clearly traumatized by the event. But I was dying to know the rest of her story and, after a brief pause, urged her to continue.

Krista wiped away her tears and broke the silence, "Haj Mirza Ali Khan said, 'My child, you are in a difficult position. A young woman alone, with such a burden of debt... It's not good, not good at all. But perhaps I can offer you a way out. Your husband is not here, and no one knows when he will be back, but I can be your great ally. I have a cousin who is a high-ranking intelligence officer. He has his ways of finding out things... very useful things. He can get information about your husband's situation in Rasht; they have informants working with the Russians.'"

Krista continued, "Even though I knew I shouldn't trust him, I was desperate. Despite my suspicions about his motives, his words made me hopeful. So I asked, almost pleading, if he could find out about Arash and if he could really help us.

"He nodded and brought his face close to mine, almost sniffing me. He smiled, flashing his gold teeth, and said, 'Yes, but such assistance comes at a price. You understand what I am offering, don't you?'"

Krista's voice quivered. "I asked him the price. He leaned back, gave me a long look as if assessing me, and asked, 'Have you heard of *sigheh*? It's a temporary marriage, perfectly acceptable. If you agree to be my sigheh until your husband returns, I will forgive your husband's debt.

"'It's a simple arrangement. You get the comfort and protection you need, and in return, I help you with your husband's debt and provide you with information. Think of it as a mutually beneficial agreement.'"

Krista uttered the words so quietly under her breath that I almost couldn't hear her. But I had heard enough and struggled to maintain my composure.

"What a pig!" I blurted out.

"And Sohrab, this man smelled so bad," Krista added, "a mix of this musty cologne, sweat, and the stench of onions he must've had for lunch. It was overwhelming, suffocating almost. I couldn't breathe. I knew I had to endure it, to sit there and not show how scared I was. But inside, I was screaming to get away, to be anywhere but there."

I couldn't believe it. Haj Mirza Ali Khan was a devout and respected elder, a pillar of the bazaar community. I was so angry I wanted to punch a wall. Maybe Arash's absence made me feel I needed to defend my brother's honor.

Krista visibly shuddered as she recalled the scene, "I was taken aback and could barely think straight. I met the man hoping to resolve the issue, thinking he would help me, but instead, I was trapped in a lion's den. You can't imagine how uncomfortable I was. My skin was crawling under his sweaty palm. I wanted nothing more than to pull away, to escape far away from him."

"How did you get out of there?" I asked her.

"I told him I had to think about it and needed some time before giving him an answer," she said.

Krista continued her harrowing tale, "I pulled myself from his grasp and rushed out of his office. Once outside the bazaar, I couldn't stop shaking. I was so ashamed. I worried he wouldn't leave me alone if I didn't take care of our debt to him. I thought, *'I couldn't let it come to this. I have to find another way!'*

"So you can now see why I was forced to sell the family heirlooms to satisfy him. It's also why I asked you to accompany me to Mr. Kahan's carpet shop; I didn't want to be alone with another man I didn't know."

My mind was in turmoil, and my head was spinning, unable to fully comprehend our dire situation. I told Krista, "Well, thank God you paid off all our debt to Haj Mirza Ali Khan; I'm glad you'll never have to deal with that lecherous man again."

Krista nodded and said, "Yes, Sohrab, thankfully so. But this has not been easy on me. I'm very depressed about the whole thing. And that's not all; the Russians say they won't let Arash leave Rasht until they get paid. But we have no more money and nowhere to turn. Our family has no credit with anyone, and nobody will lend to us."

I was stunned to hear we were broke and couldn't get Arash released. Then, increasingly annoyed, Krista unleashed her bitterness and frustration toward my brother.

"This is far from Arash's promise of a better life we would have in Iran. Why did he even think up this ridiculous business venture? Your brother is an engineer and knows nothing of business. He thinks he's just as good a businessman as your father was, but it's evident he is not.

"Arash left Iran in his youth and isn't familiar with how things are done here. He thinks and speaks differently and is obviously a novice at negotiating. Your brother is like a lamb dancing in front of wolves. No wonder it turned out this way. Only God can help us now."

Krista was so distraught that she retreated to her room much earlier than usual. The door clicked shut behind her, but it did little to muffle the sound of her ragged breathing, each trembling breath fighting back sobs.

As the night deepened, the house grew still—except for the sound of her quiet, broken cries that crept through the thin wall. I wished there was something I could do to take away the hurt, but all I could do was lie there in my bed, helpless.

Chapter 16

*"In peace, sons bury their fathers.
In war, fathers bury their sons."*

Herodotus

As the war took hold in Iran, the once fertile fields lay barren, abandoned by the farmers who fled the chaos. Desperate to revive our agriculture, the Iranian government doubled the price of wheat and looked towards India, hoping grain imports would sustain us.

But our future was no longer ours to control. The Allies had overtaken our country, commandeering every road, rail, and ship. They carved the Persian Corridor through our rugged terrain to support the Russian front, where the Soviets eagerly awaited military equipment and supplies.

Even America had turned its attention towards Iran, sending its first troops to our land. The United States, once determined to remain aloof from the distant conflicts tearing through Europe and Asia, found its isolationist stance shattered by the Japanese surprise attack on Pearl Harbor on December 7, 1941.

This cataclysmic event hurled the nation headlong into the maelstrom of global warfare. In the wake of this assault, the American military footprint expanded significantly, reaching into the most remote corners of the world.

Long after the British and Soviets occupied Iran, American forces began to trickle in, a slow but steady infiltration. The U.S.'s dual mission was as pragmatic as it was ambitious: to secure a continuous flow of war materials to the beleaguered Soviet front and safeguard the oil reserves fueling the Allied war machine.

The Trans-Iranian Railway, a marvel of engineering that scaled peaks and spanned vast chasms, became the primary artery for American engineers and soldiers. With urgency and ingenuity, they labored to enhance this crucial conduit for transporting goods and arms.

The arrival of American troops injected a new vibrancy into Tehran. Unlike the British, who carried the stiff upper lip and imperious posture of colonial rulers, or the Soviets, whose presence was marked by a stern and unyielding command, the Americans brought a breeze of novelty.

They came armed not just with weapons but with chocolate and cigarettes, jazz records that spun tunes of freedom and festivity, and a boisterous camaraderie that cut through the war's grim darkness like a beam of light. Their generosity and easy manners differed from the often oppressive overtures of their Allied counterparts.

However, beneath this seemingly benign layer of goodwill and alliance, currents of a more intricate agenda swirled. The Americans, ever cognizant of Iran's geopolitical significance — not only as a wartime ally but as a pivotal player in the post-war reordering — were determined to establish a robust foothold.

The British and Soviets viewed America's ambitions with suspicion and disdain. Neither welcomed the rise of a new power in this ancient land, interwoven with strategic passageways and rich in history. As the war raged on, the streets of Tehran became not just a battlefield of arms but of ideologies, each competing for dominance in this pivotal Middle Eastern crossroads.

Our skies buzzed incessantly with the hum of Allied planes. The ports, once quiet, now bustled with frenetic activity as a ceaseless torrent of metal surged northward through our arid deserts. Nearly 18 million tons of aid were sent to the Soviets, with the corridor acting as its main artery.

Yet, this monumental effort came with its own demons. Our railways and roads were seized, and our trucks commandeered. Those remaining few gasped for life, struggling without spare parts, now restricted by the Allies. Nationwide, construction projects pulled laborers from the fields, deepening our hunger crisis. Thousands of Allied soldiers, along with a sea of Polish refugees deported by the Soviets, now shared our land and competed for our dwindling resources.

Things went from bad to worse as the Soviets diverted grain shipments meant for our mouths to feed the Red Army. Our inflation soared, bloated by overprinted currency and spiraling prices. The streets of Tehran were choked with anxiety as the cost of goods rose by a staggering 500 percent within just a few years, exacerbated by hoarders and speculators.

Despite our government's heartfelt pleas for aid, the Western powers turned a deaf ear, placing the blame squarely on our frail shoulders. Promises were made, and vows exchanged, but the numbers told a different story. In early 1942, Iran reported needing 160,000 tons of wheat until the next harvest. But the British assessed our needs at only 30,000 tons.

The United States was initially sympathetic, but soon, their diplomats adopted the British disbelief in our plight and recommended that America support the British stance.

By the summer of 1942, famine spread like a malignancy across our nation. Riots became a daily affair, the unrest reverberating loudly in Tehran, aflame with cries for bread.

🐈🐈🐈

One sweltering afternoon, I found myself in the heart of Tehran, witnessing firsthand the devastation wrought by hunger spreading across the country. The city was besieged daily by riots—a cacophony of turmoil reverberating through its dusty streets, now theaters of despair.

As the sun beat down on the cracked pavement, I stumbled upon a crowd swelling rapidly at the city's main square. The mood was tense, charged with the collective agony of the starving masses. Their faces were gaunt, their expression hollow with hunger and anger. They chanted with fierce desperation, "You may kill us, but we must have bread!"

This rallying cry bounced off the walls, a lingering refrain that would not be silenced. At first, the police stood as silent sentinels, looking nervously over the crowd. Their initial restraint was apparent; a thin veneer of calm barely masked their underlying dread. They clutched their rifles tighter as the crowd's chants grew more insistent. Then, without warning, the tension snapped like a brittle twig underfoot.

A bottle hurtled through the air, shattering against the cobblestone with a resounding crack that sliced through the cries for bread. In that instant, pandemonium erupted. The police, their nerves frayed to breaking, responded with a volley of gunfire. The sound tore through the air, brutal and deafening.

I ducked behind a crumbling wall, my pulse racing as screams filled the air and people scattered in every direction. Moments ago, the square had buzzed with the desperate voices of the crowd; now, it echoed with the anguished cries of the wounded and the grieving.

I escaped the mayhem in the square, horrified by the sight of the fallen. I later heard that several hundred fell that day, their blood staining the street, a tragic reminder of the price paid when the pleas of the hungry are met with bullets instead of bread.

As I made my way home, the stark contrast between the streets of Tehran and the sheltered walls of our house weighed heavily on my mind. Outside, hunger and unrest had left the city stretched to its breaking point. But inside, we held onto the fraying pieces of normalcy. My family had been fortunate. Our circumstances had shielded us from the challenges many faced. Though we rationed like everyone else, my family's connections allowed us access to supplies others could only dream of.

In our Tehran home, we were like an island in a turbulent sea, buffered from the waves of starvation and suffering that eroded the lives of the average Iranian. This peculiar insulation, born more of circumstance rather than any merit of our own, lent an almost surreal quality to our existence as the streets outside resonated with the hollow footsteps of the needy and dispossessed.

When I got home, Krista was in her room, as she often was these days, withdrawing from the world beyond our walls. I couldn't wait to tell her what I had seen.

Krista glanced up from the window where she sat, her expression weary and distant.

"Have you been out again?" she asked, curious.

"Yes," I replied, sitting down beside her. "I saw more than I ever wanted to."

"Tell me," she said. "Tell me what's happening out there."

"The city is falling apart," I began. "People are starving, Krista. They're so desperate they're rioting for bread. Today, I saw a crowd… and then I heard gunfire."

She turned to me, her eyes widening. "Gunfire?"

I nodded, the memory still fresh, the crack of shots echoing in my ears.

"The police opened fire on the crowd. Many were shot. It was terrifying. There's so much suffering; it feels like we're only holding on by a thread."

Concern flashed across Krista's face as she said, "Sohrab, you shouldn't go out like that anymore; it's too dangerous. What if something happened to you? It's hard to imagine everything happening out there while we're inside the mansion, pretending life is normal. But nothing is really normal anymore."

She sighed, her shoulders slumping, "It's heartbreaking to think that all we can do is stand by and watch."

In the following weeks, an unsettling calm descended as British and Soviet troops marched through the city, their boots thudding heavily against the pavement. These foreign soldiers, sent to keep the peace, now patrolled with rifles ready, guarding against further outbreaks of violence.

The foreign occupiers could no longer ignore the desperation they helped foster. Huddled in urgent conferences, they leaned on one another for a solution—too late for those who lay motionless on the streets, but a glimmer of light for those who still survived.

Finally, the United States, Britain, and Iran signed a Tripartite Food Agreement, with the Allies agreeing to it more out of fear of losing their foothold in Iran than concern for our suffering. Soviet wheat first trickled in; then British and American aid followed, though sluggish and barely enough to stave off the worst. As grain finally began to reach the hands of the starving, a new terror emerged—a typhus epidemic.

In Tehran, and especially in the south of Iran, death knocked on door after door. The southern region of Iran, already struggling with a harsh climate and less access to relief efforts, faced compounded hardship. The British, who controlled the south, mismanaged the harvest, preventing food from reaching those in need.

And so it went, a land rich in history now impoverished by circumstance, a people caught in the churn of greater powers, their suffering etched into the lines of hungry faces, their lament drowned out by the clamor of war.

Chapter 17

"The spy who survives is the spy who never gets noticed."

Ian Fleming

Ravenshadow was the code name of the German special agent in Tehran who considered himself the "Lawrence of Arabia" of the war in the Middle East. He and his cadre of German agents who had parachuted into Iran, aided by pro-German Iranian sympathizers, organized an extensive fifth-column movement. They were to ensure that the Iranians would welcome the Afrika Korps with open arms when they came storming in. But instead of the Afrika Korps, the Allies poured into Iran, forcing the German spies to quickly go to ground.

For nearly two years, Berlin received no word, no sign of life, from the agents it sent to Iran. Then, they resurfaced right under the noses of the Allied troops. They frequently moved to avoid detection, sowing seeds of tribal unrest and jeopardizing the security of Allied convoy routes. Trains were derailed, bridges were blown to pieces, and Russian naval ships in the Caspian sunk. When not on a mission, Ravenshadow hid in plain sight in Tehran amid the hustle and bustle of the capital city.

The moon hung low in the Persian sky, casting an ethereal glow over the rugged landscape where Ravenshadow led his saboteurs through the rocky terrain, their footsteps muffled by the desert sand. His team consisted of skilled operatives carrying a satchel with explosives and other tools.

The explosives were a deadly concoction, carefully designed to create maximum damage. They contained a mixture of nitroglycerin and RDX, enough to obliterate bridges, derail trains, and disrupt the rail transport network crucial to the Allies' war effort. German intelligence supplied them with detailed maps and blueprints indicating the vulnerable points along the railway line.

As they reached the strategic location, Ravenshadow assigned each saboteur their task. One planted the explosives on the tracks while another wired them to a detonator. Their synchronized efforts ensured a devastating impact. They worked swiftly and silently, their gloved hands expertly handling the materials.

But as they camouflaged the last explosives, the silhouette of British sentries emerged against the horizon. Ravenshadow's pulse surged, adrenaline flooding his veins as he signaled his team into the cover of a nearby rocky outcrop.

Heartbeats pounded loud in the stillness of the desert as they lay breathless, the sentries' boots crunching gravel perilously close. Moment by moment, the sentries' footsteps faded, swallowed by the vast, indifferent desert.

Ravenshadow and his team remained motionless, concealed in darkness, until they were sure of their escape. It was a brush with capture, a fleeting dance with fate — they had vanished like specters at the edge of dawn. As the danger receded into the night, Ravenshadow allowed himself a thin, cold smile. They planted the seeds of chaos, unseen and unheard, ready to bloom into a firestorm that would ripple through the corridors of power.

Communication with Berlin was essential for the success of their operations. In a hidden cave nearby, Ravenshadow set up a makeshift radio station with a powerful shortwave transmitter. He tuned in to the Radio Berlin Persian evening service, receiving their instructions in coded news broadcasts. The coded messages were transmitted precisely at 8 p.m. local time, ensuring the Germans received their orders without arousing suspicion.

As the days turned into weeks, the German saboteurs faced numerous challenges. The rugged terrain, treacherous weather, and the ever-present danger of being discovered tested their mettle. But they persisted, driven by their unyielding loyalty to their cause.

Meanwhile, the Allies were baffled by the audacity and precision of German sabotage. British commanders and soldiers discussed the difficulties of confronting and stopping the frequent attacks on the railway. They couldn't understand how the Germans managed to repeatedly evade their grasp.

Unbeknownst to the Allies, tucked away in the Zagros Mountains' hidden recesses, German paratroopers discovered refuge with the nomadic Qashqai people, known for resisting British influence in Iran.

The Qashqais had a long-standing conflict with British forces and viewed the Germans as potential allies in their opposition. This tribe was anti-Shah, well-armed, and disgruntled by British encroachment on their territory, so the Qashqai offered critical support and shelter to the Germans. This collaboration created a complex network that provided a secure haven for the saboteurs to regroup and strategize.

Incidentally, Ravenshadow's delicate first assignment upon arrival in Iran was to befriend the pro-

German chief of the Qashqai and deliver a personal gift from Hitler – a golden pistol and thousands of gold coins. Laden with explosives and gold, the paratroopers from Germany persuaded the Qashqai to join forces in a rebellion against British rule.

Through their collective efforts, Ravenshadow and his team continued their campaign of sabotage, dealing significant blows to the Allied war effort. The Germans exploited the element of surprise, striking when and where the enemy least expected. Ravenshadow's ability to outmaneuver the Allies left them dumbfounded. In the heart of Iran, the presence of the German spy cast a long and ominous pall, challenging the might of the Allied forces and leaving them on edge.

In the quiet of his lair, Ravenshadow recorded his inner thoughts:

In these turbulent times, this journal serves as my anchor, a means to document the struggle, the aspirations, and the cruel circumstances we face. This is a record of a personal journey and a monumental clash of ideologies and cultures, played out in Iran's hidden alleys and grand bazaars, a land caught between ancient traditions and the inexorable march of modern warfare.

Recording in this journal is a task I undertake with a heavy heart. However, it is necessary to have tangible evidence of my activities to justify my past actions or explain future outcomes arising from our clandestine plans. Time marches on relentlessly. Autumn has arrived, yet the German forces remain ensconced before Stalingrad. This is not to cast aspersions or display ingratitude toward our valiant soldiers. Rather, it is a manifestation of the deep-seated worry and fear for our mission that compels me to write.

With each day, our existence becomes more fraught. The encroachment of German troops compels the enemy to enforce stricter regulations, reminiscent of martial law. The British Consul in Isfahan was overheard saying to an acquaintance that "99 percent of the Iranian population supports the Nazis, and the remaining one percent accepts our money only to betray us." Each advance by our forces thus heightens our peril.

Fortune smiled upon me yesterday as I listened to the Führer's speech. After being deprived of his voice for so long, hearing him speak was nothing short of spiritual succor. I pray these writings will serve as evidence of a singular belief that might still fall short of the collective faith of the millions of our men battling on the Eastern Front. Still, this is more than the tale of one individual; it is a chronicle of a people's struggle for their destiny. I stand on the periphery of the war's events but may be in its throes tomorrow. Let us hope for such a day.

Gradually, I find myself unraveling the enigma of engaging with the Persians. They are willing to embrace extreme risks, even the ultimate sacrifice when approached with respect and understanding. Their faith in the might of Germany, in the Führer, and the invincible spirit of German power is nothing short of mythical. Such conviction stands tall, impervious to the onslaught of enemy propaganda. This zealous belief remains unswayed by riches or threats. It is a fragile faith, one that we Germans might unwittingly dismantle if we fail to tread with caution.

Amidst this complex backdrop, the Melliun Movement, a fervent assembly of nationalists, aspires to consolidate all Iranian factions and societies with a singular vision: the liberation of their motherland. They regard the National-Socialist regime of Germany as a pivotal ally in their crusade against the imperial ambitions of Bolshevik Russia and the Anglo-Saxon nations.

A list of traitors to Iran is being compiled – Jews, Bahais, Communists, and all those who have thrown their lot in with Britain or Russia, not to mention former Iranian ministers who have abandoned their homeland's interests. In due time, when the German Army sweeps through Iran and assumes governance, these traitors will be apprehended and delivered to justice.

🐈 🐈 🐈

The British knew little about the German spy, Ravenshadow, beyond his code name. Pursuing Ravenshadow had become an all-consuming obsession for Lieutenant Colonel Edward Leslie Spencer, a gallant British Royal Artillery and Defense Security Officer in Tehran. Capturing the German agent had become Spencer's personal crusade.

Before the world was engulfed in the mayhem of the Second World War, Spencer's life was markedly different, contrasting to the person he became in the streets of Tehran. Born into a modest family in the heart of England's countryside, E. L. Spencer's childhood was steeped in the pastoral beauty of his homeland. His father, a veteran of the Great War, imbued in him a sense of duty and a deep respect for the military. Spencer's mother, a schoolteacher, nurtured a love for literature and history.

As a young man, Spencer attended a prestigious military academy, where his keen intellect and natural leadership qualities distinguished him. Not only did his military prowess set him apart, but Spencer also had a voracious appetite for knowledge and fluency in several languages, including Persian, which he learned out of sheer fascination for Persian poetry and history. He was introduced to the beauty of the poetry through Edward FitzGerald's translation of Omar Khayyam's *Rubaiyat*.

Spencer joined the Royal Artillery upon graduation, where his talents were quickly recognized. But his life took a dramatic turn with the outbreak of the Second World War. Spencer was assigned to intelligence work, where his unique skills were desperately needed. His ability to blend into different cultures and his linguistic skills made him invaluable.

Before his assignment in Iran, Spencer had served in various European theaters, where he witnessed the brutality of war. These experiences left an indelible mark on him, shaping his worldview and solidifying his resolve to fight against the tyranny that threatened to engulf the world.

Spencer's arrival in Iran was more than a military assignment; it was a journey to the land that had long captivated his imagination. But the romanticized vision of Persia he once held was now juxtaposed with the grim realities of war and espionage. In Tehran, Spencer navigated a complex web of politics and intrigue. He developed a network of informants and allies, some found in the most unlikely places.

Twice, Spencer came tantalizingly close to apprehending Ravenshadow, only for fate to intervene unkindly at the last moment. On one occasion, under cover of a moonless night, Spencer and his select operatives encircled the old quarter of Tehran where time stood still, its narrow alleys keepers of past secrets. Intelligence, gathered from a clandestine meeting with a double agent and confirmed by intercepted communications, led them to a decrepit building rumored to be Ravenshadow's temporary lair.

As they moved silently, communicating with hand signals, Spencer felt the thrill of the hunt. They were close, closer than ever before. Suddenly, a figure darted across a rooftop, spotted by the faint glow of a distant street lamp. Spencer's heart hammered in his chest. With a jerk of his head, he motioned his team to encircle the building. Tensions were at a fever pitch as they crept forward, closing in on their prey. The scent of victory hung in the air.

But then, the unthinkable. A bloodcurdling shriek shattered the night's stillness. A stray cat, startled by their approach, erupted from a hidden nook, its shadow grotesquely magnified on the wall by a flickering lantern. The team, momentarily thrown off guard, instinctively flinched. In that heartbeat of distraction, a figure – a phantom in the darkness – melted back into the labyrinthine alley, swallowed whole by the ancient stone walls. Spencer roared in frustration, the sound thundering off the buildings like a wounded beast. The prize, so close, had slipped through their grasp.

Several months later, the British officer was offered another chance to capture the elusive spy. This time, the hunt led them to the heart of Tehran's bustling bazaar. Spencer, disguised as a local merchant, his face obscured by a carefully cultivated beard and a heavy turban, blended seamlessly with the throng. Scattered like invisible threads, his team weaved through the crowd. The intel was that Ravenshadow would meet a contact beside the fountain at the heart of the market, exchanging vital information that could shift the situation in Iran.

As Spencer maneuvered through the multitude, his focus fixed on the fountain, he felt the pulse of the crowd change. Tension crackled in the air; it was almost time. But just as he spotted a figure that matched Ravenshadow's description, a commotion erupted. Two men, arguing over a perceived insult, their faces contorted with rage, came to blows, their altercation escalating into a full-blown brawl. The market erupted, with vendors and shoppers scattering, a human storm that Spencer fought to navigate.

In the pandemonium, he caught a glimpse of the German. Their eyes locked for a brief, electric moment, sending a jolt through Spencer. In that split second of turmoil, Ravenshadow disappeared.

Spencer pushed through the multitude, desperation clawing at his throat. He reached the crowd's edge just in time to see a weathered wooden door swing shut on an ancient alleyway– a mocking invitation to a chase that had once again slipped through his fingers, leaving Spencer grasping at air. He leaned against the rough-hewn door, the sounds of the marketplace fading into a dull roar.

The hunt for Ravenshadow became an obsession, a personal vendetta. The German was more than an enemy agent; he embodied Spencer's frustrations in this war. He seemed always one step ahead, as if he could read Spencer's moves before they were made.

The British officer was sure that Iranian police and pro-German sympathizers in the Iranian military were protecting Ravenshadow. This complicated the cat-and-mouse game and made each failed attempt sting with the bitterness of betrayal. Many nights, a frustrated Spencer found himself alone, contemplating the *"Moving Finger,"* his favorite *rubai* (quatrain) of Khayyam:

> *The Moving Finger writes; and, having writ,*
> *Moves on: nor all thy Piety nor Wit*
> *Shall lure it back to cancel half a Line,*
> *Nor all thy Tears wash out a Word of it.*

Each botched effort at capturing Ravenshadow only strengthened Spencer's resolve. Like Omar Khayyam's verse, which speaks of time's irreversible flow, Spencer understood that the past was unchangeable and that there was no room for regret. Sleepless nights spent poring over maps and intel reports left him exhausted. The weight of a double life, a world away from familiar shores, pressed on him. But Spencer wouldn't yield. The fire to capture Ravenshadow burned ever brighter, an unrelenting force that propelled him forward.

CHAPTER 18

"War is deceit.
A single spy can cause more damage than a whole army."
Prussian King Frederick the Great

Oberkommando der Wehrmacht (OKW)
High Command of the Armed Forces

Berlin, 1943

A discernible tension hung in the smoke-filled room of the German high command. Field Marshal Wilhelm Keitel, his face creased with worry, broke the silence. "Mein Führer, the situation on the front is dire. We must consider unorthodox strategies."

Adolf Hitler, seated at the head of the table and burning with an unsettling fervor, responded sharply, "I demand not just strategies, Keitel, but a plan that can turn the tide of this war. We must strike them where they least expect."

Heinz Guderian, the general known for his panzer tactics, leaned forward, "There's intelligence, albeit fragmented, suggesting the Allied leaders might meet in Tehran in the fall. We have heard Churchill has named this conference 'Eureka.' Imagine the impact if we could disrupt that meeting…"

Hitler's interest was piqued. "How are you sure it will be held in Tehran?"

Guderian replied, "We know from intelligence reports that Stalin is afraid to fly by plane, so our informants in Baku tell us the Soviets are preparing a special carriage for him to travel by train from Baku to Tehran."

Hitler waved him on, "So what's your plan, Guderian?"

Guderian continued, "An operation to assassinate Roosevelt, Churchill, and Stalin. With them gone, the Allied forces would be headless, possibly open to negotiating peace on terms favorable to us."

Keitel interjected, "But Mein Führer, our intelligence has been flawed, as in the case of the White House error."

A trace of irritation crossed Hitler's face.

Keitel continued, "As you recall, our agents were diverted to America because our decipherers misinterpreted the intercepts and reported 'Casa Blanca' as the 'White House,' allowing Roosevelt and Churchill to meet in Casablanca, Morocco, unharmed. We tried to be too smart for our own good."

Guderian chimed in, "We've learned from that mistake. This time, we will have contingencies in place. We have agents on the ground behind enemy lines who were in hiding but have recently reestablished communication. We will use a large truck bomb; it will destroy the conference room in the Russian Embassy where Stalin wants the meetings held."

With ruthless determination, Hitler declared, "Then it's settled. Make the necessary arrangements, and ensure no detail be overlooked."

As the officers nodded in agreement, the room filled with a renewed sense of purpose, though one tinged with the desperation of their situation.

Tehran, 1943

As Tehran became a key channel for Allied logistics, its streets morphed into a kaleidoscope of cultures — foreign troops — Russian, British, and American — patrolled side by side. The city, once a bustling hub of Persian culture and commerce, now throbbed with military urgency.

This fusion of global influence was most evident on Naderi Street, where cafés that once served only the finest Persian teas and delicacies now also offered homesick soldiers rations of tinned beef and vodka.

The street had grown quieter under the watchful eyes of Allied occupiers. The usual clamor of commerce and conversation was muted, replaced by the mechanical hum of military vehicles. The vibrant market stalls were fewer, and those that remained were often half-empty, as curfews and rationing took their toll on daily life.

However, the spirit of Tehran's citizens persisted, and their resilience was visible in how they adapted to the new circumstances, finding small ways to reclaim their city under occupation.

Ravenshadow sat alone in his dimly lit safe house on Naderi Street, a haven from the tension outside. He had received a message from the German high command, transmitted through a clandestine radio signal that crackled to life in the dead of night. The message was haunting in its simplicity.

His heart pounded as he reread the message to make sure: *Operation Nightshade. Target: Russian Embassy. November 30.*

While this cloak-and-dagger play was going on, the Tehran Conference loomed. The planned historical meeting of the Allied leaders was not just a strategic summit but a beacon of hope for an Allied victory.

Churchill, Roosevelt, and Stalin were scheduled to meet in Tehran, and the Nazis were determined to end their alliance by any means necessary. The espionage efforts surrounding this conference were intense, with every side aware that the outcome could decisively influence the direction of the war.

The German plan was diabolical. The Nazis intended to blow up the Russian Embassy, where the leaders were gathering. It was a desperate bid to plunge the Allies into chaos and perhaps secure more favorable terms for peace as the Nazi regime teetered on the brink of collapse.

Ravenshadow faced a daunting obstacle. Allied checkpoints choked the city, making the transport of explosives a near impossibility. But disobedience was unthinkable. His loyalty to the Fatherland was absolute, transforming him into a cold, efficient instrument of its will.

In the following weeks, Ravenshadow scoured Tehran and even as far as the outskirts of Rasht, attempting to procure the materials he needed for his plan. He moved discreetly through the city's bustling markets, holding clandestine meetings with contacts who could help him secure the explosives.

But each step was a gamble, as the Allies had eyes and ears everywhere. He eventually found what he needed: stocks of ammonium nitrate fertilizer piled up in an abandoned warehouse outside of Rasht.

The German agent was fortunate to find such an amount unguarded at the edge of what used to be a farm. Because of its dual-use nature, ammonium nitrate was closely regulated during the war to prevent it from falling into the wrong hands.

The Allies had commandeered all available transport for the war effort, forcing the Germans to improvise with a mix of bribed drivers and stolen vehicles. The psychological toll was immense. With a precision known only to a seasoned spy, Ravenshadow orchestrated a covert plan to have the fertilizer transported discreetly to a predetermined location outside of Rasht.

The stakes were high, and the logistics were nightmarish. Ravenshadow divided the cache into shipments, delivered by separate operatives to the city's outskirts. From there, alternate routes were planned into southern Tehran for storage until the fateful day.

Some couriers didn't even know the contents of the cargo they carried. With each delivery that began to trickle in, Ravenshadow was brought closer to the grim reality of his mission.

The major obstacle to the scheme was that large trucks were needed to transport the heaviest bags of explosive materials. The usual automobile or horse-drawn carriage couldn't handle moving loads of that weight, leaving the German agent grappling with how to carry out his planned mission, which, if successful, could turn the tide for the faltering Nazi regime.

CHAPTER 19

"If you can't feed a hundred people, then feed just one."
Mother Teresa

Haidar returned to Tehran from Qazvin for a visit, and it was a joy to see him and hear the stories he told of transporting food supplies for the Allies. His dark skin contrasted with something that caught my eye: a shiny British army watch - a rare 1940 Vertex, an unmistakable signature of British luxury. As I was intrigued by watches, he noticed how much I admired his.

Haidar lifted his wrist closer to my face and asked, "Impressive, isn't it?"

"It's beautiful. Where did you get it? "I asked as I kept looking at it.

"It's from smugglers bringing goods from Iraq into Iran. I buy a trinket or two from the smugglers whenever I drive near the Iraqi border," he winked.

The description of that route was enchanting. Driving on rugged terrains, surrounded by vast stretches of golden deserts, the roads bordered by sparse vegetation, and the mirage playing tricks on the horizon sounded exciting.

"Take me with you the next time you go," I blurted.

Haidar raised an eyebrow, amused, "Actually, I'm heading there next week to deliver supplies. You can return to Qazvin with me, and we'll set out from there."

The prospect thrilled me. Arash was still in Rasht, and Krista trusted Haidar, so I prepared to go with her blessing. I asked Karl if he wanted to come along, but he said his father was worried, stirred by rumors that the Allies were looking for German spies in the countryside. He forbade him, fearing Karl may be mistaken for one.

We reached Qazvin without incident, thanks to Haidar's permit, which allowed us safe passage through the checkpoints. When we got to my cousin's house, Abbas came to the door and was surprised to see me, unaware of Haidar's offer for me to tag along. We sat cross-legged under a dim light on the living room's weathered carpet to drink tea from the samovar.

After Haidar explained why I was there, my cousin seemed worried.

"I'm telling you, Haidar, it's too risky for Sohrab to ride as your passenger. The Allies are watching the roads from Qazvin to the border. You know no passengers are allowed, only drivers from here on out. They won't be lenient if you get caught."

Haidar rubbed his chin, "But I've traveled these routes countless times. It won't be a problem."

Abbas replied, "Maybe because you were driving alone, and besides, Arash would never forgive me if something happened to Sohrab."

Abbas could see my disappointment. He thought briefly and then suggested to Haidar, "There may be a way for him to accompany you without raising suspicion. Why not call him your *shagerd shoofer*? (Driver's assistant).

Haidar thought it was an excellent plan, "Exactly. You won't be considered a passenger if you're a shagerd shoofer. It'll give you a purpose, a reason to be on that truck. And that's what we need."

All this talk made me nervous, "But do I look the part? They'd see right through it."

Abbas replied, "Leave that to me."

He left the room briefly and returned with an old mechanic's coat stained with oil and dirt. He held out a handful of oily nuts and bolts that he removed from one of the pockets.

"Wear this, and keep these in your pocket," he commanded.

Haidar chuckled, "Look at him. Now that's a proper shagerd shoofer. If we're ever stopped, pull these out."

I was no longer nervous but excited, "It's genius, Abbas. But I need to know how to act the part."

Haidar instructed me, "Just remember, keep your head down, act busy, and always keep those nuts and bolts within reach. They're your ticket to a convincing story."

And with that, he turned to my cousin and said, "Don't worry, Abbas; I promise I'll keep him safe."

The next afternoon, we went to a storage facility the Allies had set up outside Qazvin. Haidar loaded the truck with bags of grain for transport that evening.

As the truck rattled along the rugged path, Haidar, gripping the wheel with a tightness that mirrored his emotions, glanced sidelong at me, pointing to people walking around searching for food.

"You know, it's not the fault of these poor souls," he began, his voice rough with suppressed emotion.

"The Allies… they've brought this hunger upon us."

Haidar took a deep breath and added, "A friend of mine works at a morgue in Kermanshah. He tells me the streets are filled with semi-naked and starving people. Fifteen deaths a day, Sohrab, just from hunger and disease."

I swallowed hard, struggling to comprehend it all. "That's horrifying."

"And that's not all," Haidar continued, his voice heavy.

"In February, typhus hit the city. The hospital was shut down because so many doctors and staff were infected."

Silence filled the truck's cabin, broken only by the engine's rumble and the sheer magnitude of the truth we faced.

I murmured, "They've plundered us, but what can we do? We are helpless."

Upon hearing this, Haidar stopped the truck on the side of the road and turned to me, "Remember that day in Tehran years ago when the cat stole my lunch, and I choked its neck to get my cheese back?"

I laughed, "Yes, I remember I warned you that you would get sick eating the cheese that had fallen to the dirty joob."

With a sly smile, Haidar said, "And do you remember the time we went to Qazvin to see the damage caused by the bombing and how I swore that I wouldn't let my countrymen starve because of an imposed war?

"Well, these sons of bitches — the Russians and the British — are like that damn cat, trying to steal our lunch and send it to their troops up north. But if I have to, I will pull the grain, piece by piece, from their filthy throats and feed my people. Remember Sohrab Khan, I told you no one takes my lunch unless I offer it."

I asked, "But how will you do what you say?"

With a prideful air, he replied, "I've already been doing it. For the past few months, whenever I load up the truck with bags of grain, I first drive to nearby villages where the people are starving with nothing to eat. I drop off just enough bags so they go unnoticed by the occupiers. Don't you see how ridiculous it is that I must steal the food they are stealing from us? That's why I travel mostly at night."

What I considered an adventurous trip got even more exciting when he told me about the wild scheme he had devised. And I didn't know why he called it stealing; it's not stealing when you take back what's yours. It was brilliant.

He pulled back onto the road, and as the truck rattled along the uneven path, Haidar leaned over to me, his voice barely above the engine's hum.

"Sohrab Khan, do you see how he moves? Strong and steady through the roughest paths," he said, patting the dashboard affectionately.

"I named my truck Rakhsh after Rostam's legendary steed. Like his horse, he's more than just transport; he's a companion warrior in my quest."

I watched Haidar; his expression was defiant and proud. The companionship and safety Rakhsh offered him in the lonely night hours created a unique bond between the warriors. It was almost as if I could hear each creak and groan Rakhsh made tell a story—of journeys past and the secrets they had shared.

I could see how, when everything looked uncertain and our fates hung by a thread, Rakhsh gave Haidar a semblance of control over his destiny. He considered himself fortunate that he could move around and carry what was needed where it was needed most.

Haidar added, "It's not just about our survival, Sohrab. It's about our dignity, about resisting the humiliation of our people being overlooked in their time of need. This truck, my Rakhsh, is part of me and my contribution to our fight."

I nodded, understanding the depth of his commitment. The rugged and reliable truck was much more than steel and engine; it was a lifeline and, for Haidar, a symbol of his patriotism and strength. As we continued our journey, distributing the much-needed food, I saw not just a man and his truck but a modern-day Rostam riding his Rakhsh across the land he so fiercely loved and vowed to protect.

The truck swerved slightly as he navigated a pothole, his hands steady on the wheel.

"You know the story, Sohrab, that when Rostam first saw Rakhsh, he knew the horse was meant for great deeds. There's a tale that when he asked the herdsman the price of the stallion, he responded, 'If you are Rostam, mount him and defend the land of Iran. The price of this horse is Iran itself and mounted on his back; you will be its savior.'"

Haidar said proudly, "That's what I aim for with my Rakhsh here. These roads we take, the food we distribute to the starving villages—it's my way of mounting my steed to salvage what can be saved for our Iran. Maybe it's not on the battlefield with a sword. Still, every bag of Iranian grain that we can use to feed our people instead of Russians is a slap to their faces in defense of our land." As we continued driving, the desert night shimmered with the heat from the blistering day. Stars overhead pierced the sky with their intense glow as the winding dirt roads faded into obscurity.

"We have only the cover of night," Haidar said, turning off the truck's headlights and navigating the path with a familiarity that spoke of many such journeys made before.

Driving at night was a strategic move, keeping us hidden from the omnipresent British sentries. The villagers knew not to use lights, aware that the Allies patrolled the roads. Haidar had a system in place, choreographed to the finest detail, and each step was perfectly in sync with the villagers and their *kadkhoda* (the village leader).

In each village, a man stood by the farthest edge, his silhouette barely visible against an endless sky and a moon that seemed indifferent to our mission.

Haidar would give a quiet whistle—a soft, trilling sound mimicking the nightjar's call. The man would respond in kind, signaling that the coast was clear. We would drive into the village, silent as wraiths, and unload the grain sacks into waiting hands. Village men would then disperse, each carrying a bag on his back, like nocturnal ants scurrying off with their treasure. Women and children would watch from a distance with quiet gratitude.

All the while, Haidar would stand tall, overseeing the operation with a vigilance that belied his fatigue. The silence of the night was broken only by hushed footsteps and the occasional distant bark of a dog. And then, just as swiftly as we arrived, we'd leave, moving on to the next rendezvous.

We carried the weight of the villagers' hopes, helping them reclaim some of their lost dignity and standing fast against the starvation inflicted by those who took over our land. It felt like righting a wrong that was carved into the soul of Iran.

Seeing my hungry countrymen in these villages sat uneasily on my conscience, reminding me of the arbitrary lines between privilege and privation. The war, with its cruel indifference, segregated our people into those who suffered directly and those who observed from a distance. I found myself on the privileged side of this divide, and while I was grateful for my situation, my heart ached with a heavy sense of guilt.

It was a bit before midnight when we distributed all the bags Haidar could afford to give away without the

Allies counting them missing. We then took off to deliver the remaining bags to the train station near the Iraqi border for shipment north to Russia.

Haidar, to combat fatigue, had started using opium. The initial harmless puffs had turned into a nightly ritual. That night, he was more stoned than usual, his eyes glazed and unfocused.

Suddenly, the glare of a searchlight blinded us. It was a British sentry point. A rush of adrenaline surged through me as Haidar headed straight for the barrier gate.

"Haidar!" I yelled, "Stop the truck!"

But he seemed detached, entranced by the glaring light. With my heart pounding, I grabbed the steering wheel, swerving hard to the right. We barely missed the British soldier, who dove out of the way, his face a picture of shock and fear.

"Brake, Haidar! Brake!" I screamed.

We crashed through the gate, finally coming to a halt less than a hundred meters ahead. The sudden jarring crash brought Haidar back to his senses, but it was too late. A hail of bullets tore through the back of our truck.

"Drive!" I cried. The engine roared to life, and we were off, leaving the checkpoint far behind. Haidar shut down the headlights as we continued driving in total darkness.

Several kilometers down the road, a dimly lit signboard reading *Ghahveh Khaneh* (coffeehouse) appeared, marking a popular truck stop. Haidar sped up, swiftly turning into the lot.

"Quickly, into the coffeehouse," he commanded.

Sweat dripped from our foreheads as we found a table, attempting to appear nonchalant. I could see Haidar's hands shaking.

"Act normal," he hissed.

But it was only a matter of minutes before the British soldiers stormed in. They located our truck by the bullet holes in the back. They found Haidar's permit inside the truck under the driver's visor and swiftly identified him using his picture. I watched, helpless, as they took him away for interrogation. The weight of the situation sank in. Our adventure had turned into a nightmare.

The coffeehouse door banged shut behind the British soldiers. Truckers leaned over their tables, murmuring among themselves. The tension was so thick you could cut it with a knife. Haidar was gone, taken for questioning. I was left in a purgatory of doubt, wondering what to do.

I stumbled back into the biting cold of the desert night, clutching my coat around me. Midnight had passed, and the sky was an ink-black canvas studded with the icy sparkle of stars. A few meters away, a fire burned. Some Iranian truckers were huddled around it, their faces dancing in and out of the flickering light.

"Come sit, join us," one of them called out.

I hesitated but then joined the circle, settling down beside the fire. The flames cast shapes on the sand like wayward spirits in restless motion. The trucker's faces were etched with the fatigue of long-haul journeys and the stress of wartime uncertainties. They spoke quietly, sharing stories of border crossings gone wrong, encounters with the authorities, and families and homes they had left behind. I told them about Haidar, how we nearly ran over a British soldier, and Haidar's being taken away for questioning.

A couple of drivers offered me a ride in the morning. "You can't just sit here, waiting," they argued.

It was a tempting offer, but I declined. I needed to find out what had happened to Haidar; I couldn't abandon him. I thanked them and focused on the fire, mesmerized by the dance of its flames.

The night unfolded with agonizing slowness, each minute stretching into eternity. Finally, as dawn began to smear light across the horizon, I saw a trio of figures approaching.

Two were unmistakably soldiers; between them walked Haidar. My heart leaped. As they neared, I saw a document in one soldier's hand, which Haidar had signed during his questioning. The guard handed it to Haidar, informing him, "You'll have to pay a fine for the damaged barricade and endangering military personnel. The fine will be addressed to Abbas Ahangar, the truck's owner, in Qazvin."

I was surprised to see the soldiers were Indians with turbans. I knew the British called their country "British India" —a term, I suspected, must have chafed at their spirits. I wondered why people, themselves shackled by colonial chains, were willingly fighting under the banner of their subjugators. Serving the power that denied them their freedom was a baffling sacrifice.

Under British colonial rule, India contributed one of the largest volunteer armies to the British war effort. Far from their homes across the Indian subcontinent, these men were deployed as soldiers in a land equally foreign to them, a necessity dictated by the tides of war.

Stretched thin across multiple fronts, the British Empire used its colonial resources, deploying troops from India to critical areas to maintain control and secure oil supplies. The Middle East, with its pivotal importance for oil and as a logistical gateway to the Soviet Union, was such a region.

Indian troops were adaptable and seasoned. Their presence was not merely a matter of manpower but of strategic foresight. The British, conserving their own for battles closer to Europe's heartland, found in their

The Harmless Necessary Cat

Indian subjects the capability and the resilience to manage the difficult conditions.

The Indian soldiers, despite being thousands of miles away from their native soil, stood as both overseers and unwilling participants in the larger game of war—a game orchestrated from far beyond the deserts of Iran by those who charted the maps of conflict with lines that often disregarded the human elements involved.

The soldiers who brought Haidar turned to leave. Haidar stepped forward, his face exhausted, his eyes vacant.

"I was worried for you. I kept thinking of Abbas and Arash. They would never forgive me if something happened to you," he murmured.

"Let's go into the coffeehouse, Sohrab. I'm so hungry," he said softly.

I asked, "Didn't they feed you in lock up?"

Haidar replied, "They offered me something to eat, but I would rather starve than accept food from the occupier's hands."

Haidar resented the foreigners for offering him food they were stealing from his people.

When we came out after we finished eating, Haidar went to retrieve the truck and told me to buy some fruit from the nearby vendor for our return trip. I tried to be as inconspicuous as possible, knowing that Haidar would return with the truck at any moment.

Out of nowhere, a British soldier stepped before me, blocking my way, barking in English, "Papers, show me your papers!"

I acted startled, hoping to shake him off. I gestured that I did not understand what he was asking, mumbled a few Persian words, and attempted to sidestep him. My heart raced, every beat urging me to flee.

"Stop, you stop right there!" the soldier shouted, his eyes fixed on me.

I quickened my pace, desperately trying to disappear into the crowd. His hand clamped down on my shoulder, stopping me in my tracks.

"I said show me your papers!" the soldier repeated, his grip tightening.

When I thought I was done for, an Iranian policeman stepped in.

"He no speak English," the policeman said in broken English, gesturing towards me. "I translate."

The soldier's skeptical eyes met mine, "Ask him what he's doing here."

Taking a deep breath, I played my part. "I am a shagerd shoofer," I said in Persian in response to the policeman. I reached into my pocket and produced a few nuts and bolts, displaying them as evidence.

"Truck driver's assistant," the policeman translated for the soldier.

The soldier, slightly mollified, nodded. But before I could place the items back in my coat pocket, he forcefully grabbed my hand, turning it over and holding it tightly. He studied my clean fingernails, which was not something he would expect from a driver's assistant.

"Who are you, and what are you doing here?" he asked suspiciously.

I was terrified. The situation rapidly deteriorated. Trying to save me from the soldier, the policeman pleaded, "He's just a kid; let him go."

Another British sentry came forward and said, "Let's take him away for questioning; he may be a spy."

I nearly soiled myself when I heard that. My heart was thumping like a drum. I feared the worst. From the corner of my eye, I saw familiar faces from the night before – the truckers. They closed in around us, their anger radiating.

One shouted, "Leave our boy alone!"

The encroaching crowd grew restless, their voices growing louder and their behavior more aggressive. The policeman warned the soldiers that he couldn't stop the mob if they didn't let me go.

The loud honk of a truck horn pierced through the commotion. Haidar had returned. Seizing the moment, I bolted toward the safety of the truck. Just as a soldier's hand clamped onto my shirt, a firm hand pulled me away.

"Run!" a familiar voice yelled.

The last thing I heard as I jumped onto the truck was the cacophony of angry shouts and curses aimed at the now beleaguered British soldiers. The truck's tires screeched in a desperate bid for distance. Each heartbeat resonated with the feeling of a narrow escape and the dread of what could have been.

Haidar glanced over, his eyes widening as if asking a thousand questions. I begged him, "Drive, Haidar, just drive," I panted, my eyes still on the side-view mirror where the scene of my almost-arrest receded into the distance.

"Get us out of here," I yelled.

As we sped away, I caught my breath, grateful for the truckers' timely assistance. Haidar stared ahead, his eyes glazed, hands tightly gripping the wheel. We were jarred and shaken but free and moving toward home.

The looming threat of the British sentries faded into the distance, swallowed by the sprawling, rugged landscape that unfolded before us. The sky brightened, turning the dusty windshield gold, and the weight of the night's dangers began to lift. With each mile we traveled toward home, the once-dark road shimmered with the promise of a safe return.

Chapter 20

"The only way to get rid of temptation is to yield to it."

Oscar Wilde

When we returned to Tehran, Haidar wanted to leave for Qazvin after a brief rest and some dinner. But Krista insisted that he spend the night and go in the morning, to which Haidar agreed.

Later that evening, Mr. Mayer arrived at our home. I was surprised to see him and hoped Karl would be with him, but not this night; Mr. Mayer was alone. I didn't get a chance to greet him as he rapidly walked past the courtyard and went up the side stairs to my father's study, which was now used as Krista's office.

🐈🐈🐈

Even though Krista felt the weight of Arash's absence, thoughts of Franz comforted her. Whenever he could visit, his presence was a welcome relief from the solitude that filled her evenings. Lately, she found herself craving the simple touch of another human being, the warmth of shared breath.

Despite her routine of reading morning scripture and occasional church attendance, Krista wrestled with desires contradicting her beliefs. The teachings were clear and foreboding: "Sin is crouching at the door…Live by the Spirit, and you will not gratify the desires of the flesh."

The flesh, ever weak and insistent, murmured promises of fleeting pleasure and temporary escape. Krista knew, deep within her soul, that surrendering to these desires was wrong. What, then, makes a person yield? Is it the insatiable hunger of the flesh or the aching void within the spirit seeking solace?

She prayed for divine assistance to avoid succumbing to the immediate. Yet, words seemed distant in the quiet of her room. Temptation tugged at her, its seductive allure twisting logic and blurring the lines between right and wrong: *Why continue to suffer alone when comfort is so near? Isn't God's grace abundant and forgiving?*

These thoughts mingled with the image of Franz and his subtle flirtations. Krista struggled to think about the consequences of her burgeoning feelings. A battle waged between her devotion to God and the primal human need for connection.

God has cheated you, the tempter's voice cooed softly, exploiting her weakness.

With all you are suffering, why not feel good for a while? What does it matter anyway?

With each passing day, the mental and emotional strain carved deeper grooves of justification in her thoughts. Krista began to see God not as the sovereign she owed her allegiance to but as an absentee who left her to fend for herself. She felt abandoned, and while trapped in the realm of conflicting passions, this was the evening her internal turmoil would peak.

Franz's offer to come by "just to talk" played on her mind, a constant tug-of-war between caution and desire. It was a moment of reckoning, but she had made her choice in her temper tantrum with the Almighty. Her decision did not ambush her; she walked into it with open eyes, believing this was the only way to feel whole again. Her heart had its reasons.

Franz caught Krista seated near the window, eyes lost in the distance. He asked her, "Krista, what happened? You look unnerved."

"It's Arash… and everything else. It feels like I am drowning in a sea of troubles," Krista sighed.

Franz went and sat beside her, "I understand. These are trying times for all of us."

Krista added: "But it's not just the war, Franz. It's Haj Mirza Ali Khan, one of the people from whom Arash borrowed money. He proposed to make me his sigheh in exchange for forgiving Arash's debt. He made me feel like a whore. I feel so trapped, so… humiliated."

Franz gently touched her arm, "So uncivilized, a temporary marriage? It's just legalized prostitution. The things they think of. But don't worry, you're not alone in this. I'm here, and we'll figure something out."

Krista told Franz that she had already repaid Haj Mirza Ali Khan's debt by selling whatever she could find of value. She divulged that she needed to pay off the Russians but couldn't gather the amount they demanded.

Krista was evolving from a helpless wife, anxiously waiting for news of Arash, to a woman increasingly drawn to Franz. The shift had been gradual yet undeniable. Once light-hearted and filled with dry wit, their interactions began to carry a deeper, more charged undercurrent. Jokes and playful banter had now given way to lingering looks, unspoken desires, and a tension neither could ignore.

With Arash gone, Krista found herself adrift. Once the epitome of composure, Krista grappled with desires she had long buried under the facade of a dutiful wife. Soon, she would be crossing lines, which she never thought she would. But Krista would do it willfully, with almost rebellious intent.

Franz's strength and decisiveness contrasted with her disappointment and frustration with Arash. It wasn't just physical attraction that pulled her towards Franz. With him, Krista felt a rush of excitement, a vibrant spark in a world that had grown dark and uncertain. It was exhilarating.

She confessed, "I'm conflicted, Franz. It's all too much; it's been hard for me alone. Without Arash, I don't know what I'm going to do. And I know I shouldn't…, but I'm scared of these feelings…"

Franz was caught off-guard. He cautioned her, "Krista, what feelings? …"

Krista interrupted him with a sudden, impulsive kiss. Franz was taken aback but responded with an enthusiasm that surprised them both.

"For the first time in a long time, I feel safe," Krista said softly.

The events of recent months had eroded her confidence, leaving Krista lost. But in her confusion, this act of defiance offered her a semblance of control—a precious commodity in the chaos that had become her life.

In this clandestine encounter with Franz, she found an anchor in her bold indiscretion. It was a moment where she could wield power, bask in the allure of being desired, and dance on the edge of the taboo.

In that space, the decision was Krista's alone to make. And make it, she did. She plunged into the depths of a forbidden night, seeking a fleeting moment of comfort where her raw, unfiltered need was satisfied. With every kiss and caress, she was reclaiming herself. With Franz, she discovered a part of herself she had forgotten—a woman who could love fiercely and without restraint.

In the dim light of the study, the air was filled with the lingering scent of passion and the faint trace of cigarette smoke. Franz and Krista, their bodies entwined on the couch, were caught in a moment of serene intimacy, a world away from the turmoil surrounding her life outside the room's four walls.

The glow of the cigarette in Franz's hand cast a soft light on his face. He took a long drag, then turned to Krista, asking, "Even if you managed to get the money, how would you safely deliver it to the Russians to secure Arash's release?"

Krista exhaled slowly, racing through the possibilities in her head.

"Maybe we could use Haidar? He drives a truck for the Allies and has all the necessary permits if he is stopped at checkpoints. Just by chance, he is staying here tonight and planning to leave for Qazvin tomorrow morning."

Franz sat up slightly, the cogs in his mind visibly turning.

"That could work. But, Krista, if I can find a way to procure the funds, I might need a favor in return."

Intrigued, Krista stubbed out her cigarette and faced him. "What kind of favor?"

"I've been trying to get building materials to my workers near Rasht," he explained, his voice taking on a tone of urgency.

"Transportation has been a nightmare. Maybe Haidar could help move these materials once he delivers the money to the Russians. It's just a few bags, but every little bit helps to repair the damage to the railway line."

She thought for a moment and answered. "If it helps get Arash back and aids your work for the railway, I don't see why not."

Franz said, "Good. If Haidar is here tonight, why wait? Let's get Arash out of the clutches of these Russians as soon as we can. I will try to bring the money you need in the morning. I'll be here before Haidar leaves. I can explain what he needs to do for me then."

Krista was elated and couldn't believe that Franz could help. After all, it was a lot of money, and she wondered for a second how he would be able to get it by morning. But she decided she didn't care and kissed him in thanks.

As they lay there, the room filled with the soft crackle of burning tobacco, Krista knew that she had made an alliance forged not just in shared desire but in her need to navigate the treacherous waters surrounding her.

Her desperation had blurred the lines between right and wrong. In the aftermath, the rush of illicit pleasure quickly faded, replaced by an overwhelming sense of guilt. The sweet whispers of temptation turned into bitter accusations. But having justified her actions in her mind, Krista felt no remorse.

Chapter 21

*"The supreme art of war
is to subdue the enemy without fighting."*

Sun Tzu

I was curious why Karl's father was alone with Krista in her study for that long. I wondered what they were doing, so I stealthily went up the stairs and stood outside the study to see for myself.

I peered through a crack in the door and witnessed what I thought was an intimate moment between Krista and Mr. Mayer. It looked like he was saying goodbye to her as they sat on the couch.

His touch lingered upon her hand, his voice murmured comforting words in German, "*Liebe Krista, mach dir keine Sorgen, ich werde mich um dich kümmern.*" I had learned enough German to understand the gist of it. (Dear Krista, don't worry, I will take care of you).

Then Mr. Mayer gently kissed Krista's hand and got up to leave, and I rushed back down the stairs so he wouldn't see me. Once he was gone, I couldn't wait until the morning to ask her about their conversation. I cornered Krista immediately, wanting her to shed light on their late-night meeting.

Tears brimmed in her eyes, and a weighty silence followed. While I nervously waited for an answer, my thoughts spiraled wildly. Could it be? Was she entangled with Karl's father while my poor brother was being held against his will by the Russians in Rasht? The idea of Krista betraying Arash disgusted me.

She paced the room, wringing her hands, and then delivered the news she had been holding onto, "You know the Russians won't let Arash leave Rasht until they get paid. After the debacle with Haj Mirza Ali Khan, I had nowhere to turn, so I confided in Franz," she hurriedly added, her voice shaking.

"He's offering help. Just tonight, he told me he'd manage to secure the funds."

I raised an eyebrow. "Mr. Mayer? How would he have that much money…"

Krista interrupted, a bit annoyed, "He's coming tomorrow morning with the cash. I know it's peculiar, but we're desperate. I've agreed to accept his help."

Krista didn't need such questions answered as long as she could get his money.

She then sat down and continued, "Sohrab, there's something else I haven't told you. It's about Arash. Back in Germany, a few months after we began dating, he started having heart palpitations. It was so sudden and alarming. We consulted Dr. Schmidt, a renowned cardiologist we met with in Berlin."

She paused, taking a deep breath as if to steady herself.

"Dr. Schmidt diagnosed Arash with angina pectoris. It's a condition where the heart doesn't get enough blood and oxygen. It was quite serious, and the doctor prescribed nitroglycerin. It helps to relieve his chest pains."

"Krista, why didn't you tell me this before?" I asked with frustration.

"Arash is reserved about personal matters, especially his health. He believes showing vulnerability might be misconstrued as a sign of weakness, a dent in his masculinity, so he didn't want anyone to know," she replied.

Krista folded her hands in her lap, her fingers intertwining nervously.

"It was right after Arash's diagnosis when he proposed to me. It was so sudden, almost impulsive. He took me to dinner in a fancy restaurant near our home and said, 'Life is a fleeting illusion. We must seize every moment we're given together. Why delay our love?'

"You know your brother well; he is very persuasive. I could hear the urgency in his voice, a subtle tremor that betrayed his fear. I saw through Arash's facade. His bravery was a mask, hiding what was gnawing at him."

Krista's voice wavered as she continued, "But now, confined in that hotel in Rasht, like a criminal under house arrest, I'm worried for him. We brought a supply of nitroglycerin from Germany, knowing it might be scarce here in Iran. But he didn't take enough for an extended stay in Rasht. I doubt he will find any there. The thought of him alone, without his medicine... it terrifies me."

I found myself at a loss for words, realizing the full extent of Arash's dire situation. Although I knew he was under house arrest, the fact that he was confined to a hotel had made it seem less severe. Now, I understood just how serious his predicament was.

Krista continued while unshed tears glistened in her eyes.

"You know how Arash is. He can't control his emotions and sometimes gets easily stressed. This situation he finds himself in is exactly what he needs to avoid. What if his heart..." her voice trailed off, unable to complete the thought.

I told her, "But Krista, don't worry. The good news is you said Mr. Mayer would bring the money. That's all the Russians want, right? Then they will let Arash go. And once he's back, we have his medicine here."

The obvious seemed to calm her a bit. Then I asked, "But tell me, how will we send the money to Rasht?"

Krista replied, "We're lucky I insisted Haidar stay tonight. He can do it, and he's trustworthy. His permit to drive trucks for the Allies will allow him to reach Rasht without delay or suspicion. He can give the Russians the money and return Arash to us since they have confiscated his car. I will also send some nitroglycerin with Haidar so Arash can have it if he needs it."

It sounded like a well-thought-out plan. I hoped to see Arash soon and was thankful for Mr. Mayer making it possible. While worries for Arash and our family's plight still consumed me, there was also a welcome relief. What could be better than Karl's father helping us?

How misguided my concerns had been, thinking Krista had betrayed my brother. And, after all, we had come to know that Mr. Mayer was an honorable man.

The following day, at the break of dawn, Krista, Haidar, and I nervously waited for Mr. Mayer in front of our house. He arrived with a suitcase containing the money and handed it to Krista, who gave it to Haidar to load onto his truck.

I couldn't contain my emotions, so I turned to Karl's father and spat out, "Mr. Mayer, It's humiliating. These Russians are treating this like a ransom. They can only do this because they can. I wish something could be done to rid ourselves of them!"

He probably was trying to make me feel better when he offered, "Sohrab, I know you address me as Mr. Mayer out of Persian politeness and respect for elders, but please call me Franz. It's less formal; besides, with all that is going on, you are the head of the Ahangar family until Arash returns."

I looked up to him and appreciated that he treated me as a grown man, not just a kid.

Franz continued, "I know the sting of such humiliation all too well. After Germany surrendered in the Great War, the French did the same to us—all those demands we could not satisfy. The reparations they imposed asked Germany to pay for war damages when Germany had nothing to give. Even so, we paid, and they made us pay until just a few years ago. They destroyed our economy. Just as you now want your country's glory restored, I also wanted our Fatherland's brilliance to shine again, but what could we do? Our country was ruined; the only way we could resist was to fight our battles in the shadows."

I was puzzled. "In the shadows?"

He took a deep breath, looking down the empty street.

"What I mean is that when faced with overwhelming force, sometimes the best way to resist is through subtle acts of defiance, unseen but deeply felt. During those hard years in Germany, some resisted by keeping our culture alive and simply working quietly to rebuild with the promise of a better future. It's not always about fighting back with guns or fists. Sometimes, the most potent weapon is resilience and the refusal to be broken."

As he spoke, I realized Franz was talking about the Haidars of Iran, men who selflessly carried the weight of the nation's dreams with the satisfaction that each of their small acts was a rebellion against the occupiers. I had been a witness to such selflessness just a day earlier.

Franz paused, placing a reassuring hand on my shoulder. "Not all battles are fought for victory - some are fought to tell the world that someone was there on the battlefield. Tomorrow I have to travel to inspect the damage to the rail line near Arak. Lately, in most cases, sabotage has been the cause of the damage. I've seen the impact that your fellow Iranians have had, working in the shadows but resolute. It's as if they're silently telling the Allies, 'You may control our land, but not our spirit.'"

Franz leaned closer, looking me in the eye, "I cannot tell you how to free Iran from the grip of these occupiers, but I can tell you this: if you hold onto your identity and your culture, they can never truly conquer you."

I nodded, absorbing Franz's words. After all, he had also grappled with formidable foes in his past, much like the ones confronting us now. His talk of resilient defiance illuminated a path forward for me. It also made me grateful that our country had birthed men like Haidar.

Chapter 22

*"Death is nothing,
but to live defeated and inglorious is to die daily."*

Napoleon Bonaparte

The following day, relieved that Haidar was on his way to deliver the funds to the Russians, I decided to spend my afternoon with Karl, who was alone now that Franz had gone to Arak.

The air was still as I walked towards his house, my heart racing excitedly. I was eager to share my encounter with the British soldier a few days back. And I had more news: his father was helping us get Arash home.

When I finally reached his house, the reception was far from what I had envisioned. The light in his living room window revealed a troubled face. I stepped inside as Karl opened the door, oblivious to what he was going through. I blurted out, "Karl, you won't believe what happened to Haidar and me on our trip! The British thought..."

"Not now," he interrupted, his voice shaky. "I can't."

Confused, I took a closer look at him. His eyes were rimmed red. Something was terribly wrong. "What is it?" I asked with a sudden urgency.

Karl sighed, pointing to the letter on the table. "The postman delivered this letter a few hours ago. It's from my mother," he choked out.

"Is it about your uncle in the Luftwaffe? Is he alright?" recalling Karl's previous concerns.

He shook his head. "No, it's not him. It's about…my childhood friend. You remember asking me about Albert?"

I nodded. "Yes, of course. What about him?"

"Just read it," he said, his voice heavy with dread.

"I can't read German that well, you know," I reminded him.

He took a deep breath, holding the letter tightly as he read, translating the words for me:

My dear Karl, I hope this letter finds you well despite the circumstances under which it is written. In your last letter, you asked about Albert. My heart aches to tell you the truth I have long withheld for fear of how it might affect you.

One afternoon, before you left for Iran, while I was tidying up your father's study – a room you remember that he always kept locked and private – the door had been left ajar, which was quite unlike him. Driven by curiosity and the uneasy feeling building in me for some time, I ventured inside.

In the quiet of that room, amidst the many papers and books that defined your father's world, I found a stack of documents hidden inside a drawer. These were not ordinary papers but were official correspondence. What I read on those pages shook me to my core.

Among these documents was a list of names and addresses, including Albert's and his mother's. I discovered the circumstances under which they abruptly left our service. This was no willing exit, as your father claimed. He somehow discovered they were Jewish and may have played some role in their sudden departure.

But the most devastating blow came when I saw the names of my dear friend Sophie and her brother Hans Scholl at the bottom of the list. I never imagined your father could be involved in something like this. When I learned the truth, it shattered whatever faith I had left in him.

It pains me to burden you with this, but you are old enough now to understand our world's complex realities. Your father, the man you have looked up to, has embraced a path I despise and cannot follow. It is a truth I wish no mother had to reveal to her son.

Karl choked out, tears dripping onto the parchment, smudging the ink. A cold wave washed over me. My mind raced, trying to process the heaviness of the revelation. Karl's hands clutched the letter tightly as if trying to wring out a different truth from its pages. He drew a shuddering breath before continuing.

Your father has threatened me with dire consequences if I interfered or tried to sway you against him. His love for you is real, but it is a possessive love that fears losing control. He brought you to Persia to keep you close, under his influence, away from the ideologies that he claims corrupt the youth of Germany — Be careful, my son. Keep your wits about you and remember the morals I taught you. Trust in your heart.

If ever you find yourself in doubt, look inside and remember who you are, independent of your father's legacy. Please destroy this letter when you read it; if he finds out you know the truth, he may react badly. Always with you in spirit and love, your mother.

The room was stifling as Karl was clearly in agony, feeling betrayed by a father he so admired. The words in the letter painted a very different picture. The revelation that his father, a man he revered, was involved in such things sent a tremor down Karl's spine.

Terror-stricken, he asked me, "Do you know what this means?"

I had a blank look, as I didn't know the implications of having your name on a list, so Karl explained.

"These lists," he said, "they are the Nazi's tools of terror. They meticulously document the names and addresses of those they deem a threat or undesirable: Jews, political dissidents, and anyone who dares to challenge their twisted ideology. The regime sends people on these lists to prison or worse!

"I can see how Aunt Sophie and Hans, who were outspoken activists against Nazi oppression, would be monitored by the regime, but why would Albert's name be on the list?..."

Karl paused, his gaze growing distant as he tried to unravel the mystery. Then, a chilling memory surfaced – a conversation with his father years ago. He had innocently asked why Albert was circumcised, not understanding the significance at the time. His father's expression had been unreadable then. Karl's stomach tightened with dread, realizing he had unwittingly betrayed his childhood friend, exposing Albert's Jewish heritage. It all clicked into place, the pieces of a devastating puzzle snapping together.

"Oh no!" Karl gasped, his voice trembling. "My father... he was complicit, sealing the fates of innocent people. How can I be the son of a man who sympathized with Nazis? How could he have done such a thing? He has shattered our family's honor. I feel so ashamed of who I am!"

Confused and unsure how to comfort him, I placed my hand on his shoulder and asked, "So why was Albert's name on the list?"

Karl's breath caught, and he felt like the air had been knocked from his lungs. "It was something I didn't understand then," he said slowly, his voice thick with regret. "In Germany, Jewish boys are circumcised. The day I asked my father why Albert was different, I had no idea what I was revealing: that Albert was Jewish. And I... I handed him that information without realizing the consequences."

I struggled to find the right words to comfort him. It was clear that his mind was torn, grappling with the conflicting emotions of his heritage—his deep love for his father and the overwhelming revulsion at the horrific act he appeared to have committed.

The weight of his family's sullied reputation pressed heavily upon him. A shame that was suffocating and crushing. Karl was agonized by a barrage of unanswerable questions. How could he continue to bear the name of a man who epitomized the very essence of cruelty he had come to despise?

Karl dropped his head into his hands, deep in thought. After a long silence, I said, "But Karl, maybe your mother is mistaken about what happened to Albert. How can your father be a dishonorable man? He is helping to pay the ransom to get Arash back from the Russians. Just yesterday morning, he brought a lifeline for my family – a large sum of money we sent to Rasht with Haidar. Don't overthink it. If you ask your father when he returns, I'm sure he will be able to explain."

Karl didn't respond. He just sat there numb, shaking his head in grief.

"What will you do now until he returns from his trip?" I asked.

"I don't know what I'm going to do; I need to clear my head," he muttered.

I asked him if he wanted to come to our house, not wanting to leave him alone at such a time.

"No, I want to rest now, but I think I'll go hunting early tomorrow morning," he answered.

Karl's plan surprised me. "Hunting? Alone by yourself?" I asked. I knew I had to be there for him. "Then let me come with you."

"My father will be in Arak for a few days…" Karl trailed off, the weight of his father's actions pressing down on him.

"I need some quiet time to think about what to do. How can I ever face my father knowing what he did?"

"Alright," I reluctantly conceded. "But promise me you'll be careful."

Karl looked at me, his eyes clouded with pain. "And you promise me you won't tell Krista or anyone about this until I figure things out."

"I swear it," I assured him.

No matter how much I insisted on staying with him or asked him to come to our house, Karl refused. He said he wanted to rest and wake up early, telling me the mountain air would do him good.

As I got up to leave, Karl unwrapped the leather band of his watch from his left wrist, pressed it into my palm, and said, "I want you to have my watch."

I didn't understand why he gave me the timepiece his uncle, the celebrated Luftwaffe pilot he admired, had gifted him.

I asked, "Why are you giving me your watch?"

Karl made it clear he wished to avoid discussing it, and his only reply was a desperate plea in broken Persian to quell further discussion. "*Torokhoda, ghabool kon.*"(I beg you to please accept).

With the recent revelation about his father, I wondered if his uncle's heroism had been transformed into something darker in Karl's mind. Did he now see his uncle not as a gallant aviator but as a dreaded Nazi? Was this keepsake a tarnished emblem, a relic of a legacy he no longer wanted to remember?

He was very emotional, but who wouldn't be after learning what he had just discovered about his father? So, I didn't want to argue with him any further about his watch. I thought I would return it to him when he was feeling better and would accept it back.

When I got home, an unbearable emptiness washed over me. I knew I had to keep my promise, and this news locked away even from Krista.

Throughout the night, I couldn't sleep. Whenever I closed my eyes, I was haunted by Karl's revelation and the torment brought upon him. I would see Karl's troubled expression and hear the tremor in his voice as he read his mother's devastating letter.

Each toss and turn became a restless, anxious dance, waging a losing battle against the unease that refused to let me sleep. The sheets twisted around me as though mirroring the knot tightening in my gut. Even in the stillness of the night, his dejected voice echoed relentlessly in my ears, impossible to silence. I prayed for dawn, clinging to the hope that it might bring peace.

As dawn broke, the first rays of sunlight filtered through my window, casting long streaks of light on the floor. Outside, the city of Tehran was slowly waking up, its bustling streets oblivious to the unrest within me.

The early morning sun's heat was nothing compared to my burning anxiety to see Karl. I was worried for him and had an overpowering need to do something. I wanted to get there before he went hunting to accompany him and ensure he was all right.

But when I arrived, his home was eerily quiet. I had come too late to join him; he had already left for his hunt.

I went to his downstairs neighbor's apartment and knocked on the door to see if they knew what time Karl had left, thinking maybe I could catch up with him. An old man opened the door, and when I asked if he had seen Karl earlier this morning, he raised a quizzical eyebrow and answered with disbelief.

"Haven't you heard? *Almaniyeh* (the German) was cleaning his rifle last night, and it… it went off."

I was dumbstruck and stood there numb as if I had not heard his heartbreaking answer. I asked again.

He said, "Didn't you hear me the first time? The German boy is dead! They took his body to the morgue early this morning when the housecleaner found him."

My world crumbled. I knew Karl. He was meticulous, especially with his rifle. Karl was too skilled to make such a mistake. I couldn't accept his demise was just an accident; it was a silent scream, a final act of defiance against a legacy of hatred he could not accept nor escape.

The struggle between familial loyalty and moral disgust eroded Karl's mental stability. I believe he saw himself as irrevocably tainted by his father's sins, a burden that led him to take his own life, crushed under the weight of a painful truth.

Tears welled in my eyes, and I let out a heart-wrenching scream. Seeing my distress, the old man tried to comfort me by patting me on the back, but I just wanted to get out of there and ran back to my house.

My promise to Karl just yesterday to say nothing, which felt like a burdensome shackle, had now become a harrowing truth I had to divulge to Krista.

But first, I went to my room to collect myself; too much had happened, and it was hard to process. In my thoughts, I was swept back to that day in Qazvin, inside the café. Karl had posed a haunting question to Abbas: "Would one kill for honor?"

Abbas replied, "One would not just kill but also lay down his life for it."

Ironically, with one shot, Karl had done both. Not as Abbas had declared for honor but because of the dishonor Karl's father had brought upon him.

Karl had lived his life trapped in an illusion, loving a father who seemed to be a stranger to him. He was broken and tormented by guilt for inadvertently revealing Albert's secret to his father. How could he carry the weight of his father's transgressions? Maybe taking his own life was his way of trying to atone for the sins of his father.

After taking time in my room to gather my thoughts and overcome my shock, I went to tell Krista the dreadful news.

I could see Krista was in her study. I knocked on the door, and she looked up from what she was reading and welcomed me with a delightful smile.

"Krista," I began, my voice shaking, "I have some terrible news about Karl."

"What news?" she asked, worried.

"He's...he's... dead," I mumbled, fighting back the tears.

"Dead?" Krista asked, her expression frozen in shock. "How?"

"They say his rifle went off while cleaning it, but Karl... he knew his way around guns. I know it wasn't just an accident," I said, trembling, "Something doesn't add up."

Krista's face clouded with disbelief. "Oh no! How could this have happened? Why do you say it wasn't an accident?"

"Because of what Karl just discovered yesterday," I replied.

Krista impatiently asked, "Well, what?"

I told her, "Karl discovered that Franz is a Nazi sympathizer and was overcome with unbearable shame."

"What?… Oh no! " she protested, her voice catching in her throat.

"Nazi sympathizer? That can't be. Franz would never…"

"Karl read me a letter from his mother," I interrupted. "She warned Karl about his father."

I then told her what his mother had written about Albert and Sophie. For a moment, a heavy silence enveloped the room. Krista looked lost in thought, struggling with the magnitude of what I'd just shared.

But then, teary-eyed, she slammed her hand on the table and declared, "No! That's just hearsay! Franz and Karl's mother are estranged. People say things when they're hurt or angry. It doesn't mean it's true. It could have been anyone informing authorities about his friend.

"Besides, I've already told you that back when I lived in Germany, some of our friends and relatives joined the Nazi party, not because they believed in the cause, but to keep their jobs, not in sympathy. And I don't mean high-level jobs: I mean like teachers and municipal workers. Karl's mom must be mistaken; Franz is not like that. He can't be. It's because of his help that Arash will be coming home soon."

I didn't know what to make of it. Krista's stubborn defense of Franz struck me as odd, leaving me to wonder if there was more to their relationship than she was willing to admit. At the same time, it was equally difficult for me to believe that a man so refined and worldly could align himself with the Nazis. He wasn't a monster. I thought, *How could he wear two faces and only show us one?*

"In any case," Krista warned, changing the direction of our conversation, "For Karl's sake, we should keep this between us for now. There is no need to give life to rumors when it may all be a misunderstanding. I am unsure how, but we must contact Franz to tell him what happened."

CHAPTER 23

"Inter arma enim silent leges."
(In times of war, the laws fall silent).

Cicero

In this global arena of shifting alliances and rising tensions, ordinary German citizens in Iran were caught in the crossfire. The British and Russians initially treated the German settlers with suspicion, subjecting them to surveillance. Mistrust hung heavy as anyone with ties to Germany encountered scrutiny and strict restrictions on their movements and activities.

Some high-profile German citizens and those with questionable ties were detained, their businesses seized, and their assets frozen. Once-thriving German institutions were forced to close their doors, and German schools shut down.

The changes felt deeply personal for the Germans who had made Iran their home. The streets they once walked without fear now felt hostile, and the neighborhoods where they'd exchanged smiles with their neighbors now brimmed with hushed conversations and uneasy glances.

As the occupation dragged on, the looming threat of internment or worse forced many families to make the heartbreaking choice to flee. To leave everything behind was not just a physical departure—it was the severing of roots, the erasure of years spent building lives, friendships, and dreams in a land they thought would shelter them. Bidding farewell to the country they had come to love was difficult, but for some, remaining was impossible.

Some Germans like Franz, ever resourceful, blended seamlessly into the busy streets of Tehran. Krista, married to an Iranian and successfully integrated into the local community, stayed in the safe cocoon of her home, where her German identity slowly faded into the background.

For the Germans who remained and could not hide or blend in, the German Embassy's summer residence in Shemiran became a sanctuary. The compound's verdant gardens, with their ancient trees and flowing streams, soon filled with hundreds seeking refuge.

Inside the embassy walls, life carried on with an air of strained normalcy. Men, women, and children tried to make the best of their confinement, though the weight of impending disaster hung over them. Children played quietly while their parents whispered plans and hopes for a way out.

Delicate negotiations ensued between the British, Soviets, and Iranians, each vying to determine the fate of these German civilians. Under pressure from the Allies, the Iranian police forbade the Germans from leaving the compound. The embassy, a symbol of diplomatic order and protection, now felt like a cage for those within.

The Germans knew that time was running out. As they were still armed, they declared they would resist any attempts to detain them, invoking international law as their shield. The compound, neighboring the Turkish embassy, offered a slim hope. They quietly spoke of a daring plan to breach the wall and escape onto Turkish grounds if the Allies came for them, hoping they would hesitate to provoke a diplomatic incident with Turkey.

Finally, after grueling negotiations, a decision was made. Hundreds of women and children were granted passage to Germany via Turkey, a sliver of hope in an otherwise bleak situation. But this mercy came with a terrible cost: the men of fighting age would not be allowed to join them.

Families were torn apart as husbands, fathers, and sons were herded into makeshift camps in Basra, Iraq, for interrogation, leaving the women to fend for themselves. The separation was swift and brutal. Some women stood in silence; others wept openly as they clung to the men they feared they'd never see again.

The conditions in the internment camps were harsh for the men. The days dragged on in a monotonous haze of uncertainty, with meager rations barely sustaining them through the relentless cycle of hot days and freezing nights. No high walls or iron bars existed, but the coils of barbed wire surrounding them were a menacing enough reminder of their confinement. They had no idea how long they would remain interned or what fate awaited them. The absence of news from the outside world left them suspended in a state of anxious limbo. Still, as grim as life was for the men, the suffering awaiting the women was even worse.

The German women who were allowed to leave had to pass through Soviet-controlled zones on their way back to Germany. It was on this route that hundreds of women and young girls became victims of horrific assaults. Their innocence, their lack of connection to the atrocities of the war, offered no protection. For the Soviet soldiers, the scars of Hitler's Operation Barbarossa had cut deep, and these women became easy targets for retribution. The streets were transformed into a theater of hate, where the women were verbally and sexually abused, their spirits crushed under the weight of an unforgiving collective punishment.

CHAPTER 24

"Beware of strangers bearing gifts."

Aesop

The journey to Rasht passed without incident, granting Haidar some quiet time to sift through his tangled emotions. He was reluctant to fulfill Franz's request. Still, he felt obligated due to Franz's assistance to Krista, which left him unable to refuse.

The roads were rough in places, but his sturdy truck was well-suited for the terrain, having been maintained meticulously for such trips. Upon arrival, Haidar went to Commissar Khadeyev's office, a plain, two-story building dwarfed by taller, more ornate structures. He was escorted inside by a guard, where he was told to wait until a Russian soldier went to fetch Arash, who was under house arrest at the next-door hotel.

About half an hour later, Arash, looking tired but unharmed, walked in. A rush of relief passed between the two men. Arash thanked Haidar for coming with the money, but the guard told them not to talk to each other.

They were taken to the Commissar's office, where Khadeyev sat at his desk. Haidar handed the suitcase to Arash, who placed it on the Russian's table for him to open and inspect.

The Commissar took a cigarette out of its case, gently tapped it on the table, then placed it in his mouth and lit it before attempting to open the suitcase. Once the stern-faced Russian had taken a few puffs, he clicked open the lock on each side. After a closer inspection, the Commissar was delighted with its contents. He grinned with satisfaction as he shut the case.

Khadeyev got up from his chair and addressed Arash, shaking his hand.

"You are free to go, Mr. Ahangar, now that your debt has been paid."

Arash, barely excited, turned to Haidar and said, "Let's go."

As they left the building, he told Haidar, "I know you must be exhausted driving all this way to Rasht to do me this favor, but I can't wait to get back to Tehran, to Krista. Do you think it's possible to leave and return now? If you are tired, I'll drive."

Haidar replied, "I can't just yet. I promised Krista I would help Mr. Mayer deliver some construction materials to an area a few kilometers outside town. Once I do the job, I'll return to spend the night in your hotel room, but don't worry about me. I will sleep on the floor if I get in late, and then we can leave early in the morning."

Arash nodded, understanding his debt to the person facilitating his release. He returned to the hotel, but now as a free man. He phoned Krista on the crackling line to let her know he was released while avoiding sharing details, aware that the lines were far from secure. He told Krista they would be leaving to return to Tehran early the following day and should get there by nightfall.

Meanwhile, Haidar reached the outskirts of Rasht, where the building materials were to be picked up. The location was a secluded warehouse. From what Mr. Mayer asked of him, Haidar only expected to be transporting a few bags but was met with an overwhelming pile of twenty heavy sacks. Haidar began loading them onto his truck with a sigh, his muscles straining with each lift.

Finally, with all the bags secured, he drove to the designated drop-off point, fatigue beginning to set in. Haidar began unloading the bags, placing them near the entrance of a seemingly abandoned structure that would be their final destination.

In this isolated location, the evening was calm. The night air was crisp, and the chill made Haidar pull his jacket closer around him as he worked. The thud of each bag hitting the ground sounded unnaturally loud in the stillness of the evening, bouncing off the structure's walls. As Haidar lifted the bags from the truck, each one feeling heavier than the last, sweat beaded on his forehead, trickling down his face in rivulets. His muscles screamed in protest with each load, and he could feel his heart pounding against his chest, a frenetic rhythm that matched his growing unease.

Haidar couldn't help but wonder why Mr. Mayer wanted the bags placed in a desolate area without anyone to receive them. His words replayed in Haidar's ears: *The railway workers who will come for them usually come at different times of the day, depending on their shifts. Even though it's a desolate location, it will be fine if you leave them exactly where I tell you.*

But Haidar couldn't shake off the feeling that something was amiss, and the remote location only added to his suspicions. He paused momentarily, wiping the sweat from his brow, his lungs heaving with each breath. It wasn't just the weight of the bags that burdened him; even heavier on his conscience was the nature of the favor Krista asked of him.

After unloading almost half of the bags, Haidar decided to take a break. He sat on the pile and searched his pockets with trembling hands for a cigarette. Along with it, he also pulled out the nitroglycerin medicine Krista had given him for Arash, which he had forgotten to deliver. *I'll give it to Arash this evening when I return to the hotel,* Haidar thought.

When he finished his smoke, he flicked the remains to the ground, unaware that a spark had landed in a small tear in the sack beneath him.

Seconds later, the ground shook violently as an explosion ripped through the quiet evening. The night sky briefly turned a fiery orange as the sound reverberated through the valley. In the immediate aftermath, a dreadful, hollow silence followed the thunderous roar.

🐱🐱🐱

Arash awoke early in the morning and realized Haidar was not there. He thought maybe Haidar had returned so late that he didn't want to disturb him, deciding to get another room.

He quickly dressed and went downstairs to ask the receptionist. When he got to the desk, he was startled to see Commissar Khadeyev, with two guards alertly standing beside him. The Commissar was talking to the receptionist, but when he noticed Arash, he turned and said, "Mr. Ahangar, good morning; what a coincidence. We were just about to come to your room to talk to you."

Arash nervously replied, "Good morning, Commissar. What about?"

The Commissar responded, "Your acquaintance, the man who brought the money you owed yesterday, how well do you know him?"

"You mean Haidar?" Arash asked.

Khadeyev replied, "Yes, that's the name we have."

"Why do you ask?" Arash said.

The Commissar waved his hand, ordering Arash to continue, warning, "I ask the questions here! How do you know him?"

Arash was taken aback by the Russian's tone and answered, "Our family has known Haidar from his youth, and he is like a brother to me. I came down to ask the receptionist if Haidar might be in another room because he didn't return last night as planned. I don't know where he is. We were planning to leave for Tehran this morning. Commissar, why are you asking about Haidar? What has happened?"

Khadeyev said, "He's been found."

Arash asked, "And where is he?"

The Commissar replied, "Outside of town. There was a large explosion last night, and when we went to investigate, we found a truck nearby with his driving permit inside. That's how we know it was him. We found his remains there."

Arash stammered, "Remains?…. An explosion? What are you talking about?"

Khadeyev told him, "The bags your friend Haidar was shuttling around were sacks filled with Ammonal, ammonium nitrate, and aluminum powder — an explosive mixture the Germans use with a deadly capability. The furious blast must have killed your friend instantly. Was he working for the Germans?"

Arash felt a cold shiver run down his spine. He struggled to find his voice, the shock rendering him momentarily speechless.

"But… that can't be," a grief-stricken Arash finally managed to choke out.

"Oh, no!… Are you saying Haidar… is dead? He wouldn't… he couldn't be involved in such things."

The Commissar's expression turned grim.

"Mr. Ahangar, the evidence is quite clear. Your friend was transporting explosives, and now we need to discuss your involvement."

"My involvement?" Arash said with disbelief. "I have nothing to do with this. I swear!"

Commissar Khadeyev's face was marked by suspicion. "Haidar came here to return you to Tehran. He brought you a suitcase full of cash. He must have been running your errands."

Arash replied with desperation, "Haidar was doing a favor for Franz. He's an engineer on the railway line, so if there were explosives, couldn't they be for clearing areas or maintaining the line?"

The Commissar dismissed Arash's question and asked, "Franz, you say? That sounds German. Why didn't you mention him before? What's his full name?"

Arash offered, "Franz Mayer."

Khadeyev looked surprised and gestured to the guard to come forward so he could tell him something. Once he had relayed his command, the guard saluted the Commissar and bolted to complete the task.

The Russian ordered Arash, "Check out of your hotel room. You will now be our guest for a while. But expect much less comfortable conditions there, of course, until you are no longer needed."

Khadeyev's sudden urgency alarmed Arash.

His heart pounded in his chest, fear tightening its grip. His head spun, wondering if the Commissar meant until he was no longer needed because he would be freed. Or maybe Khadeyev had something more sinister in mind.

As they entered the building where Arash was to be held, he nervously pleaded, "I assure you, Commissar, this is a big misunderstanding."

The Harmless Necessary Cat

Khadeyev responded, "Misunderstanding? We don't take chances. Not when the railway line, the lifeline of our Soviet war effort, is at stake. We have ways of uncovering the truth; most are unpleasant unless you cooperate. You'd be amazed how soon a man can lose his resolve when tested."

Khadeyev's voice was terrifyingly calm. Arash dropped his head in despair, swallowing hard, as he was ushered into the basement of the building, with images of dark, dank cells and screams playing in his mind. The notorious reputation of Soviet tactics was well known.

Khadeyev warned Arash, "Think about your family. Cooperation could make things…easier. Otherwise, I can't promise you'll ever see them again!"

He was escorted into the interrogation room, a cold dread settling over him with Khadeyev's threats. He had heard of men disappearing into the depths of their detention rooms, never to return, or if they did, as mere shells of their former selves. Tales that haunted even the bravest.

The Commissar added, "And rest assured, we will investigate your German friend, Franz, too."

Arash interjected, "He's not a friend, just an acquaintance."

"An acquaintance, how?" Khadeyev inquired.

"Through my wife, Franz sometimes comes to parties she gives at our home in Tehran," Arash answered.

The Commissar sneered, "Parties at your home? You bourgeoisie like to mingle with fascists in your unearned inherited nests, don't you!"

Arash realized the more he spoke, the worse it got. His heart raced. He needed to let Krista know he wouldn't be coming home.

"What?…No…it's not like that. Commissar, please, I must call my wife in Tehran. She'll be worried."

The Commissar ordered, "No calls. We can't risk you alerting anyone else who might be involved."

Arash replied, "But Krista is not involved either. She is innocent!"

The Commissar asked, "Krista, your wife is German, correct?"

Arash became concerned about why the Russian was asking about his wife. He answered, "Yes,… my wife is German."

"And Mr. Ahangar," the Commissar asked, "Where did this Haidar get the money he delivered to you yesterday to pay off your debt?"

Arash's frustration and grief boiled over, and without thinking, protested, "Why didn't you care where the money came from yesterday when you gladly accepted it without any questions?"

Khadeyev leaned closer, his stare as piercing as daggers.

"Because yesterday, I wasn't investigating the suspicious death of the man who brought a suitcase full of cash for you and also happened to be transporting German explosives on an errand for you! But first, tell me about the money; how did you suddenly get all that money together?"

Arash answered, "Whatever it was, it was no errand on my behalf. But the money came from Franz. He lent us the money for Haidar to bring. At least, that's what Haidar told me."

The Commissar moved his face to within inches of Arash's, cutting through the interrogation room's dim light.

"Tell me, you lived in Germany and speak German, correct? Perhaps you even like the Germans so much that's why you married one?"

His voice dripped with insinuation, suggesting a nefarious alliance. Each question bounced off the walls, amplifying the threat behind them.

"Yes, I lived in Germany while studying there, and I speak German," he answered.

"But that doesn't mean I support the Nazis. I despise what they stand for, their cruelty, their ideology—all of it."

His plea hung in the air, a desperate attempt to distance himself from the enemy Khadeyev so clearly pictured him aligned with.

The Russian's expression remained unreadable, scanning Arash's face, trying to unearth deep secrets. The silence stretched, heavy and uncomfortable, before the Commissar finally spoke again, his words laced with scorn, delivered with an icy edge.

"And your wife was in charge of planning these parties where the fascists in Tehran gathered?"

Arash tried his best to remain calm when answering to prove his innocence, "Yes, my wife held parties…but not for fascists. Other German expatriates were naturally invited, but …we have no associations with such people. These are good Germans. If they were fascists, they would have stayed in Germany. It's all just a terrible mistake."

Khadeyev fixed on him like a predator locking onto its prey, sneering, "Good Germans? There are no good Germans; the only good ones are dead ones! Help me understand: your wife coordinates meetings at your home, and one of the guests, your German friend Franz, asked the man you considered a brother to run an errand that turned out to be deadly. If we weren't suspicious enough, you also admit that Franz gave your wife a suitcase full of money. Why would he do that if he didn't want something from you in return?"

Arash was agitated, "I don't know about any of this, except for him supplying the money."

Khadeyev paused momentarily, "Or maybe he wants something from... your wife in return? He gave the money to her, you say. That's a lot of money. You mean you never thought about this?

"All that money for your wife and not wanting anything in return? – she must be delicious," he winked and licked his lips.

The Commissar shook his head in disbelief, asking Arash, "Are you that naive? Can't you see why we would suspect you?"

The color drained from Arash's face as Khadeyev threatened, "And if you do not cooperate, don't forget what will happen to your wife, ...what was her name, ... Krista?

"Do you know what German soldiers are doing to our women back in the Soviet Union? With brute force, they are stripping our women of their dignity, inflicting unspeakable atrocities upon them.

"These are our wives, mothers of our children, and daughters of Russia. These ferocious German beasts devour whatever is in their path. Naturally, our comrades will act accordingly, using similar tactics when interrogating the German woman. Who knows, she may even enjoy telling us the truth."

The Commissar relished the thought and, for effect, smiled as if imagining the scene in his head. Then, taunting Arash, he said, "Come to think of it, after I am done questioning you, I may join my comrades to ensure she is interrogated properly."

Arash's thoughts turned from his predicament to Krista's. His world had turned upside down in a few hours, and the worst part was the unbearable fear of what would happen to her. Arash knew the Russians would be knocking on Krista's door soon, and he couldn't do anything to protect her.

Chapter 25

*"Night falls heavy, fear chills my soul,
Lost on this path, where can I go?"*

Sa'eb Tabrizi

Confined in his cell, Arash spent the night tormented by his precarious situation, dreading what awaited him in the interrogation room. His true character would soon be tested in ways he had never imagined, and his worry for Krista only compounded his fear. He knew the Russians were cunning, and it was only a matter of time before they came for her.

In the early light of dawn, Arash was yanked forcefully from his cell, his heart thrumming in a frantic rhythm of panic. He was hurled into a chamber where he felt the frigid walls close in, making it hard for him to breathe.

There was a peculiar ritual in these moments: the condemned were left alone briefly before the onslaught of torture, perhaps to reflect on their impending doom. This insidious game, played by the torturer on the victim, was the most inhumane of all.

The anticipation of horrors to come was more petrifying than the pain itself, allowing the torturers to manipulate their victims through a combination of psychological and physical stress. The Russians skillfully wove mental anguish into their methods, threatening harm to loved ones, which deepened the prisoner's agony.

Threats to Krista, alone and vulnerable in Tehran, unaware of the sinister web of suspicion that was closing in around her, agonized Arash. He couldn't bear the thought of Krista being taken by the Russians.

The idea of Khadeyev's vile insinuations about her, the disgusting glint in his eye as he spoke of her, enraged Arash. But it was a powerless rage that could do nothing to shield Krista from what was coming.

He imagined somehow escaping and warning Krista, but the thought crumbled under the weight of his grim reality. He was trapped, a pawn in a much larger game. Knowing he couldn't protect Krista or even warn her was suffocating.

Suddenly, the distant sound of footsteps quickly transformed into the heavy thud of boots drawing nearer, filling Arash with paralyzing fear. Commissar Khadeyev walked in with a guard, his face a mask of cold indifference.

Without looking at Arash, he sat down and signaled to the guard. The soldier swiftly delivered a series of stinging slaps to Arash, each reverberating through his skull, a prelude to the darker threats looming.

The forceful, demeaning blows caused Arash's lip to split and his nose to bleed profusely, with the metallic tang of his blood filling his mouth as tears streamed down his cheeks. He tried to wipe his face with his shirt sleeve as Khadeyev leaned in, his voice icy and methodical.

"You should divulge every detail, no matter how trivial you think it may be. Tell us where we can find this Franz? Where is his *rezidentura*?"

Then, while pointing to each digit on his other hand, the Russian warned, "Know that you will lose a finger for every wrong answer!"

As Khadeyev's ominous words lingered in the oppressive silence, the guard approached with a deliberate, slow stride. He placed a large leather roll with a heavy thud on the table. Unfurling it, he revealed an array of knives and small saws, each designed with a singular, gruesome purpose—to sever human flesh and bone. The cruel gleam of the blades under the dim light sent a visceral shudder through Arash.

Confronted with this horrifying display, a primal, uncontrollable fear gripped Arash. His body, betraying any semblance of composure, reacted in the most humiliating way possible as he soiled himself. It wasn't only the smell of fear that filled the room in that moment of sheer terror.

The Russian could see the torment on Arash's face. A smile curled on Khadeyev's lips as he enjoyed degrading him.

"Don't you see? Your wife is involved. She's conspiring with this Hun, Franz. With all that money he gave her, no doubt they're lovers. If you are truly innocent, as you say, and with what we already know, why would you protect them when they have been doing all this behind your back?"

Khadeyev's insinuations ignited a tumultuous storm of doubt and suspicion, tainting Arash's memories. For the first time, he entertained the unthinkable: the possibility that Krista was entangled with Franz and ensnared in a web of deceit.

Memories now twisted into sinister alignments - Krista's subtle flirtations with Franz at their gatherings, the inexplicably large sum of money he had just handed her. Arash's world was crumbling; the line between friend and foe began to blur. He swallowed, feeling the dryness in his throat. He had to tread carefully.

"Commissar, even if Franz is involved in something, it's not what you think," Arash began, his voice steady but filled with urgency.

"He's fighting against your enemy, not aiding them. He's been working to undermine their efforts."

Khadeyev's eyes narrowed. He flashed a sardonic smile and replied, "Undermining our enemies, you say? Our intelligence says otherwise!"

Arash's heart pounded, "Maybe your information is flawed in this case?"

Commissar Khadeyev's face darkened like a brewing storm at Arash's flippant response. The tension in the room grew, and the silence was deafening. With a subtle nod to the guard at the door, the tension snapped like a taut wire.

The guard stepped forward, delivering a vicious punch to Arash's jaw. The force sent searing pain radiating through his skull, and blood filled his mouth once again as a tooth loosened. Arash's vision blurred, his senses struggling to keep up with the onslaught.

Khadeyev's voice sliced through the haze, more menacing than before, "Do not think you can fool us with these tales. What do you mean?"

Arash felt the room whirling around him. As he tried to gather his thoughts, each word was a desperate plea for survival.

"Franz told me he was part of a group fighting against the Nazis from within Germany. You are both fighting the same enemy," Arash's voice quivered, clinging to the fragile thread of his argument.

Khadeyev's lost his patience. He had heard enough and slammed his fist on the table.

"Mr. Ahangar, you must confess to everything you have been involved in!"

His demand was a thunderclap, leaving no room for evasion.

Arash whimpered, "There is nothing to confess; I have told you everything I know," his body trembling as he struggled to maintain composure.

Khadeyev's words dripped with absolute certainty, "There is always more to confess. That's the nature of confessions."

The Commissar's stare probed for any hint of deception. Arash knew he was facing an adversary who would stop at nothing to extract the truth.

The foul odor that now filled the room inadvertently became Arash's reprieve from Khadeyev's malevolent intentions, at least for a short while.

Wrinkling his nose in disgust, the Commissar barked an order at the guard, "Return him to his cell and see to it that he is cleaned!"

As Khadeyev rose to leave, he cast a cautionary glance towards Arash, his voice laced with a cutting edge, "I expect answers, Mr. Ahangar. Be prepared for what's in store when you are returned for further questioning."

Arash was beyond frightened and began to shiver uncontrollably. He had difficulty breathing and implored Khadeyev with a broken voice, "Commissar, if you want answers, please, I beg you to find Franz and ask him. He will tell you we are innocent. But for now, have mercy; help me, I'm in severe pain... my chest hurts; I think it's my heart...I need nitroglycerin. Please, ask one of your doctors to examine me..."

Khadeyev snickered, ridiculing Arash, "From what I have seen of you so far, even with a strong heart, you wouldn't have a chance. It's not your heart; it's cowardice, and unfortunately, there is no medicine to cure cowardice."

Reacting to the Commissar's comment, the guard also sneered at Arash, his laughter tinged with scorn, as he shook his head in mockery. Arash's pleas were brushed aside, for innocence was no shield in times of war.

Khadeyev told Arash, "Look at you; you are breaking into pieces before my eyes. Let me share a lesson every soldier in the Red Army learns quickly about courage and cowardice. Our great leader, Tovarich Stalin, put it best: 'It takes a brave man to be a coward in the Red Army.'"

Arash was confused. What was the Commissar implying? He tried to steady his breathing. "I don't understand."

"Of course, you don't understand. You've never served in the army, have you? Do you know why Comrade Stalin said this? Let me explain," Khadeyev said.

"When the Red Army catches a coward—and we always do—the punishment he endures makes him beg for a swift end. Only a man who knows what's waiting for him and still chooses cowardice can be considered brave. You will soon discover such consequences if you continue on this path."

Terrified, Arash nervously asked, "What will you do?" Khadeyev turned to the guard and ordered Arash back to his cell. As he was being dragged away, Khadeyev pointed to Arash's left hand, adding one last stinging comment, chuckling, "Mr. Ahangar, don't worry about your wife; tomorrow, we will send her your ring finger with the wedding band adorning it. A keepsake to assure her you are alive and still enjoying our hospitality."

The interrogation took a heavy toll on Arash. As the guard roughly threw him back into his cell, a searing pain gripped his chest. He staggered, his vision narrowing, and the room spun wildly. Nausea overtook him, and he vomited violently onto the cold, unforgiving floor.

His legs gave way beneath him, and he collapsed face-first into the filth, his body trembling uncontrollably. Every heartbeat was a hammer blow, the pain intensifying with each pulse until he lay there, gasping for breath, teetering on the edge of consciousness, his world reduced to a fog of torment.

Chapter 26

"Survival makes strange bedfellows."

John Ray

It took Khadeyev only a few hours of intense questioning to figure out that Arash wasn't the brains behind the operation. The Russian commander wasn't interested in dealing with "little fish," but uncovering a German spy network, maybe even capturing the big fish Franz, would do wonders for the war effort and the Commissar's career.

Careful not to make any move that would alert the Germans, Khadeyev opted for a more subtle approach than directly confronting Krista and taking her away for questioning. Instead, he positioned an undercover agent outside the house, disguised as a local merchant selling fruits and vegetables. This way, they could ensnare Franz and other operatives if they attempted to contact Krista.

🐈🐈🐈

The night was deepening into the late hours in our Tehran home, but Arash had still not returned. Krista and I sat in the candlelit living room, the clock ticking away the minutes that stretched into hours. Every sound outside seemed like it could be him, but our expectations were dashed each time. When midnight had come and gone, we were distraught.

We stayed up a few more hours, hope and fear mingling in our silence. But there was no news, no sign of Arash. Eventually, exhaustion took over, and we succumbed to a few hours of restless sleep.

Unfortunately, the morning light brought no relief. Krista, her expression full of worry, turned to me. "Sohrab, can you contact your cousin Abbas in Qazvin? Maybe he's heard something from Haidar."

I immediately called Abbas. His voice, laden with concern, did nothing to ease our fears.

"Haidar never checked in, Sohrab. It's not like him. I don't know when they left Rasht. Maybe they got delayed at a checkpoint. When I called the hotel, no one would tell me anything. So I'm sending one of my drivers to check at Arash's hotel in Rasht, but I won't have any news until this evening."

After the call, Krista and I were at a loss, overwhelmed by the uncertainty. Then, I recalled something Krista had mentioned about Haj Mirza Ali Khan's cousin, the intelligence officer who might be able to help.

"Krista, maybe we should visit the bazaar together and ask Haj Mirza Ali Khan for a favor. I know you can't stand him, but we must see what we can find out for Arash's sake. No one else is telling us anything, especially not the Russians."

With nowhere to turn, Krista agreed. We went to the bazaar, the streets bustling with the morning crowd, but our minds were elsewhere.

I was on guard as we entered Haj Mirza Ali Khan's office, expecting him to turn lecherous at any moment, from what Krista had told me about him. He greeted us formally and could barely conceal his excitement at seeing her.

When we explained our predicament, Haj Mirza Ali Khan listened carefully and showed genuine concern.

Because Krista had not succumbed to his advances and managed to pay off our debt, he lost any leverage he thought he had. But now, by asking a favor, she would be indebted to him, and Haj Mirza Ali Khan was eager to win her over by offering his help.

"Let me see what I can do," he said with a reassuring nod. "I will contact my cousin to find out about Arash."

As we left his office, there was a faint glimmer of possibility. Relying on a man we both distrusted was a strange turn of events. Still, even the unlikeliest of allies can prove vital in desperate times.

When we got home from the bazaar, Abbas called me back as promised, his voice heavy with sorrow, "Sohrab, I have terrible news. My driver found Haidar's truck abandoned near an old warehouse on the outskirts of Rasht. The place was charred, and there were remnants of an explosion. He talked to the Gendarmerie in Rasht, and the authorities confirmed it—Haidar's dead. They don't know what happened, but they are investigating; I will contact you if I find out more. Unfortunately, there is no sign of Arash. I'm so sorry about Haidar; I know how close you two were."

The words hit me like a sledgehammer. I couldn't believe my loyal friend Haidar was gone, and all that remained were the questions of how and why this had happened. And still no news of Arash.

We didn't know what to do; Krista and I spent the evening in a haze of disbelief, grappling with the worsening situation. We sat close to the phone, anxiously awaiting any news from Abbas.

🐈 🐈 🐈

Haj Mirza Ali Khan's cousin contacted him with tragic news the following day. In a discreet conversation, he relayed to him, "They're saying the man who was working with the Germans killed himself in prison. But between us, that's what the Russians always say when they've gone too far during questioning. They likely killed him. And there's more," he told Haj Mirza Ali Khan.

"If you know the man's wife, warn her to be careful. They suspect her involvement in some way. They are hunting a German man, a railway engineer they believe is the ringleader of a spy network. She's in danger. I've seen similar cases where suspects are shipped to Siberia, many innocent. She should hide, especially now that her husband is gone; she's not safe from the Russians."

Troubled by this news, Haj Mirza Ali Khan sent a messenger to our house, requesting an appointment to see Krista. Krista agreed to meet, and Haj Mirza Ali Khan appeared respectful when he arrived. Even so, Krista asked that I be with her at all times and not leave her alone, even for a second, so I joined her to meet him in the guest room.

At first, I sensed that Haj Mirza Ali Khan preferred I not be in the room, and he subtly hinted that he wished to speak to Krista alone. But to his displeasure, Krista insisted that I stay. I didn't know then that his intention wasn't malicious but driven by a sense of discretion, thinking Krista might want to relay the sensitive news about Arash to me privately once she had heard it herself.

As Haj Mirza Ali Khan spoke to Krista, he seamlessly transitioned into fluent German, surprising us both. With my limited understanding of German, I caught fragments of the conversation, enough to grasp what he was saying.

"I am sorry to say your husband... The damn Russians...May they be cursed.... they say he was working with the Germans.... but... *"Arash ist tot."* (Arash is dead). They say he took his own life in prison. But my cousin thinks he may have been killed. It pains me to deliver this news to you. May God rest Arash's soul."

I understood the part where he said, Arash ist tot. I was dumbstruck, frozen in a moment. The words *Arash ist tot* rang in my ears. In a sudden surge of denial and rage, I yelled, "Arash is dead?" My voice broke, the words slicing through the heavy silence like a shard of glass.

Krista sighed, a sound so despairing that it drew the very breath from the room. Her shoulders slumped, and she began to tremble as if a cold wind had swept through. I watched her, helpless, unable to comfort her or even comprehend the full scope of our loss.

Krista raised her head and asked Haj Mirza Ali Khan, "Are you sure? If they say Arash was working with the Germans, then it's not true. They are making a mistake. He was dealing with the Russians; why would they think he was involved with the Germans?"

Haj Mirza Ali Khan replied, "I wish I could offer you hope, but my cousin is rarely wrong. I believe what he told me, and for your safety, you must believe me too."

We sat stunned, trying to absorb the devastating news. The air thickened, muffling the sounds of the outside world as if the house was mourning.

As Krista's quiet sobs filled the space, I collapsed on the couch with my head in my hands, hopeless and empty. Memories of Arash—flooded my mind, each a cruel reminder of what had been violently snatched away.

By speaking to Krista in her native tongue when she was most vulnerable, Haj Mirza Ali Khan bridged some of the wide gaps between them. But then he reverted to speaking Persian, delivering more bad news.

"...And - they suspect a German man, a railway engineer; the Russians hint that you might be involved with him."

Krista's face turned pale, her eyes widening in shock.

"German railway engineer?" She asked, suspecting Franz.

"But he..." Her voice trailed off as the realization hit her.

Krista tried to reassure herself, "Maybe this is all a big misunderstanding; Franz is a family friend..."

Haj Mirza Ali Khan asked, "So if this Franz is the German man they are looking for, do you know where he is now?"

Krista told him, "He said he was going to Arak for an inspection, but the day he left, his son Karl died, and Franz doesn't know; we tried to get word to him..."

Then, with a raised eyebrow, he asked, "How did his son die?"

Krista hesitated before answering, "It was an accident... he was killed while cleaning his rifle."

Krista continued with confusion, "... And Franz was helping to get Arash back from the Russians; it doesn't make sense."

He asked, "And how was Franz helping Arash?"

Krista began telling him about the ransom money, but her voice faltered midway, betraying her anxiety. A sudden, chilling memory flashed through her mind — the call from Abbas the day before, relaying the devastating news about Haidar.

She wondered whether Franz's last-minute request of Haidar had something to do with his death. The implications were terrifying. Tears streamed down Krista's face as she realized the man she had trusted and had been intimate with may have been someone she never really knew.

Haj Mirza Ali Khan shook his head firmly. "This is more serious than I thought. Did they say how Haidar died?"

Krista was dazed and didn't reply, so I jumped in. With a lump in my throat, I told him, "When Abbas called, he said one of his drivers found Haidar's truck abandoned near an old warehouse and that there was an explosion. When he contacted the Gendarmerie, they confirmed Haidar's death, but the authorities don't know how it happened."

Haj Mirza Ali Khan's expression grew concerned, his brow furrowing as he tried to process the flood of information. He paused momentarily as if struggling to keep up with the sudden revelations.

He then warned, "Franz will return once he hears his son has died. Please understand—he's probably being watched. They might already be watching this house. You must be very careful."

Krista wiped away her tears, "So what do I do now?"

He replied, "Krista Khanoom, I'm worried for your safety; allow me to arrange for some of my trusted tough men to guard your house. They'll ensure no one, especially the Russians, gets through."

Krista's breath caught in her throat as Haj Mirza Ali Khan's words sank in. She felt helpless and was terrified that the same people who had killed her husband may be coming for her. Yet, his suggested protective measures offered a small glimmer of light in the bleakness.

Krista's hands trembled, and her voice quivered, replying, "I understand, Haj Mirza Ali Khan. Your concern for my safety... means so much to me; I would appreciate it."

Attempting to comfort her, he said, in a fatherly tone, "Although the situation is dangerous, try not to worry."

Krista looked down, her mind racing with thoughts of Arash, her uncertain future, and the dangers lurking outside, "How can I not worry?" she replied, her voice breaking.

"The Russians are ruthless. They've already rounded up innocent Germans, let alone someone you say they suspect. You know what the Russian soldiers will do to a German woman. I'm terrified, and no one is left to protect me! Look what they did to Arash..."

Haj Mirza Ali Khan sought to calm her as she became increasingly troubled.

"I say try not to worry because there may be a solution. I'm sorry to bring this up at such a difficult time, but I can protect you."

Krista stopped sobbing to ask, "Bring what up? How can you protect me?"

He replied, "Do you remember the sigheh I suggested?"

A startled Krista looked at me as if to ask, *Did you hear what he just said?* Then she turned to Haj Mirza Ali Khan and replied with disgust, "What are you saying? How can you bring that up at such a time?"

He held his palms together in front of his face as he offered an apology and, with bowed head, said, "No. No. Please let me explain. I wanted you to forget I ever mentioned it. I am trying to apologize.

"I can see how, as a European woman, this tradition of ours can seem awkward and disrespectful to you, and it probably made you feel demeaned. That wasn't my intention. Instead, I am now suggesting that we light two candles with one flame to lessen the darkness of your situation and help me, too. I would have never brought this issue up at a time like this, especially while delivering such terrible news. I don't want to offend you by being too forward, but you urgently need to consider your safety. Time is of the essence if the Russians suspect you…"

Krista was exasperated and asked him, "So tell me, what are you suggesting?"

Haj Mirza Ali Khan answered, "Krista Khanoom, I'm a widower without any children. I have nobody; I spend all my time busying myself at the bazaar, even though I don't need to work. I have been a wealthy man for many years now, and because of that, I have powerful friends—friends who can protect you, Sohrab, and your property.

"You could lose everything. You know you cannot return to Germany; the place will soon be in ruins if it's not already. What's happening there now is terrible.

"I lived in your beautiful country when I was younger. My father sent me to Hamburg to study medicine, hoping I would become a doctor. But I never finished my studies. After my father passed away, I had to return to Iran early to take over the family business."

We were both confused and didn't understand what he was getting at.

Haj Mirza Ali Khan then did the most astonishing thing. He put his hand on his heart, bowed his head respectfully, and spoke in German again, saying to Krista, "*Willst du mich heiraten?*"

I understood enough to figure out he was proposing to marry her, and I couldn't believe my ears.

"Marry me, and I will protect you. Not as a sigheh, not a temporary arrangement, but a permanent one, as my wife. If you were my wife, no one would dare to harm you. No one will touch a single hair on your head."

I turned to Krista and looked at her with awe, wondering how she would react. I couldn't believe what he was asking her. We had just heard my brother was dead, and this man was proposing to his wife not even five minutes later. I thought there was no way. *How could she?*

I was grieving for Arash and frightened for Krista. It now seemed my late friend Karl may have been right about his Nazi-loving father after all, who had dragged us into his web of deceit.

Krista had every right to be terrified about what the Russians might do to her with the warning Haj Mirza Ali Khan delivered. But to my surprise, in response to him, she didn't protest or try to make an excuse to escape his sudden proposal and said nothing in return.

She sat in stunned silence, seemingly contemplating his sudden proposal. Desperate and fearful, and once repulsed by the thought of any relation with Haj Mirza Ali Khan, Krista began to view him differently.

Faced with the daunting dilemma, I saw her wrestling with the decision. I hoped Krista wouldn't act rashly by accepting his ridiculous offer.

She thanked Haj Mirza Ali Khan and gave him an answer I wanted to hear.

"Please give me some time; I can't think straight now with all that has happened. I need to mourn my husband."

Then Krista began to choke up again.

As he got up to leave, he said, "I understand. Please accept my condolences. By no means do I want to rush you, but it seems you don't have much time. If you agree to my proposal, we can have a simple civil marriage at the registrar's office nearby. It can be done very quickly."

What surprised Krista was that her feelings toward Haj Mirza Ali Khan began to undergo a subtle but profound transformation. At first, she resented him, but as danger drew closer, her perspective shifted.

In her moment of fear and indecision, she perhaps even had a begrudging respect for him. He emerged as a pillar of safety and assurance in her peril. The sense of security he provided began to erode the walls of mistrust and disdain Krista had built around him. The man she once reviled might be her guardian, her safe harbor in the storm.

Chapter 27

"Marriages of convenience are fair in love as in war."

Samuel Richardson

After Haj Mirza Ali Khan left, the room felt larger and emptier. I turned to Krista, searching for an answer.

"Krista, were you just biding time with his offer, or... are you actually considering it?"

She looked away, her gaze lost in the middle distance.

"Sohrab, it's too soon after Arash's death," her voice barely a murmur. "The thought of even considering such a proposal feels... unclean. I don't want to do it, but it's not only about me; it's about us, our home, our survival."

Her words cut deep. "There's nothing left, Sohrab. Even if we keep the mansion, we would have to sell it for money to live off of. Survival... it demands difficult choices."

I felt a pang of pain, a deep, throbbing ache. The thought of my brother's wife, whom I respected and admired, even considering marriage to a man like that, a man that old, was repulsive. I couldn't hold back any longer.

"But Krista," I said desperately, "How can you be sure he's even telling the truth? What if he's saying those things to scare you into marrying him? Isn't that exactly what he wants? To manipulate you into a corner where you have no choice but to accept? Remember how disgusted he made you feel the first day you met him?"

Krista replied, uncertain, "I've thought about that, Sohrab. But what if he is telling the truth? What then? What if rejecting him leaves us with nothing...? I'm terrified of what might happen..."

We felt suffocated by our situation, and I knew we needed to focus on what we could control.

"Then, at least, we must let my sisters know about Arash," I said to her, grasping for a sense of purpose amidst the confusion.

But Krista advised against it. She worried they would try to find a way to come home if they heard the news, and she didn't want them to get entangled in the fiasco. Krista suggested letting things settle first and then contacting them when the time was right.

Haj Mirza Ali Khan's tough guys arrived and stationed themselves outside our house for protection that evening. Krista was resolute when she did not respond favorably to his proposal. That refusal had brought a reluctant smile to my grief-stricken face, a hint of solidarity in our shared mourning.

🐈 🐈 🐈

Unsure of what to do, Krista spent the night tossing and turning, her mind racing as sleep eluded her. Unable to rest, she rose from bed and wandered into the study, drawn by the ghostly sense of Arash's presence as the city lay silent. Krista reached for her Bible, hoping to find an answer, but found none. Instead, she stumbled upon something curious — a lone key.

She tried it in the desk drawers, but none of the locks fit. Then she noticed Arash's old decorative writing slope on a distant table, long unused. Krista focused on the small lock securing its contents. She cautiously inserted the key, and the lock clicked open.

To her astonishment, she discovered a deliberately hidden letter from Franz to Arash inside. The world turns on secrets, and like the one in the letter, it would irrevocably change our lives.

The following morning, I noticed a newfound determination in Krista. It seemed that the dawn brought her clarity after a night of contemplation. However, I was shocked when she called Haj Mirza Ali Khan to accept his proposal. Less than twenty-four hours after her initial refusal, her decision was an abandonment of the grief we shared for Arash.

On the other end of the line, I could hear his voice erupt in excitement, contrasting with Krista's quiet determination.

"It's set," she said, her voice wavering. "We are going to the registry office tomorrow morning."

"What has changed, Krista?" I demanded. "How can you marry that man so suddenly?"

She looked at me, her face a reflection of the turmoil within. "Sohrab, there are things much larger than us at play," she said, a hidden tension lining her words. "I must do this—for Arash, for all of us."

But I couldn't understand, couldn't see past my grief and her perceived betrayal. "For Arash? He would never have wanted this!"

"Arash wanted us to survive, to be safe. I do it for him, for his memory. Trust that this is the only way," she implored, her plea a fragile thread in the growing distance between us.

Krista's voice took on a seriousness, "Sohrab, as the only male left, you are now the head of the Ahangar family. It's time for you to become a man who understands that we must sometimes walk paths we never imagined to survive."

She leaned closer to me, "You know, there is a poem by Goethe, a favorite poet of the Germans, something that feels like it was written just for times like these," she said, her face alight with the revelation.

"I read it a few times last night. It's called *Selige Sehnsucht* ('Blessed Longing'). In it, Goethe sees suffering as something to endure and to welcome as a visitor. It's all about accepting the bad with the good with grace. Somehow, that thought makes the darkness less overwhelming. It makes it easier for me to decide what I must do."

Her words offered a quiet fortitude against the storm lingering outside. And what she said sounded good but did little to ease my worries.

Krista continued, "Of course, I wish no harm had come to Arash. I long for a world untouched by this terrible war, where every moment feels perfect. But I'm beginning to see that such perfection is an illusion, visible only if we choose to ignore the imperfections. From now on, I refuse to surrender to bitterness. I refuse to become a captive of anger and misery. As Goethe advises, I choose a different path, one of hope, even in our imperfect situation."

I hated that Krista agreed to marry Haj Mirza Ali Khan. With the news of Arash's death still fresh, a wound open and raw, Krista's decision to marry so soon shattered any sense of stability. I couldn't understand how she could move on. Her choice diminished Arash's memory, and I sensed a growing distance, a chasm of unspoken emotions and unresolved grief that left me feeling more isolated than ever. A quiet acknowledgment that our paths were diverging.

The next day, under the watchful eyes of Haj Mirza Ali Khan's men, we formed a small procession to the registry office. There, amidst the sterile walls and the scent of ink and paper, Krista, still in mourning for Arash, consented to become a 'paper Muslim,' agreeing to convert on paper to Islam, a requirement for their marriage under Islamic tradition.

This decision must have been difficult for her, given her devotion to her Christian faith, which she had shared with me in many conversations. I was a silent witness to this joyless union—a pact sealed for protection, a surrender to the tides of necessity.

As we made our way back, I overheard Haj Mirza Ali Khan speaking to Krista in a firm and reassuring tone.

"For your safety," he said, "I will stay at the mansion. The situation is too dangerous, and I cannot leave you and Sohrab alone. My men will also keep watch until things become clearer."

His words comforted Krista but unsettled me. Now that he was her husband, I felt powerless to object. When we got home, the reality of our new world settled upon us. The mansion that once carried the laughter of Arash and Krista would now house Haj Mirza Ali Khan, its new master.

Our home, with its ornate doors and expansive halls, had welcomed countless joyous occasions. But that night, it was to become his domain, a man as foreign to its history as he was to us. Knowing he would share Krista's bed left me uneasy. The thought of this man she barely knew taking my brother's place in the room where she had once found comfort in Arash's arms was almost surreal. Haj Mirza Ali Khan entering that intimate space was an intrusion, erasing part of my brother's legacy.

Witnessing their union felt like a desecration of the past, a violation of the sacred memories I held of her with my brother. This man, with his corpulent figure and a manner as coarse as the graying bristles that adorned his face, was no match for the spirited, loving partner that Arash was to Krista.

During the night, the thin walls allowed sounds to seep through to my room for longer than I wanted to remember. Despite his advanced age, he had a robust appetite. The creaking of the aged bed under his substantial weight was a jarring soundtrack to the tragedy unfolding in the next room.

Haj Mirza Ali Khan's labored breathing, punctuated by grunts of exertion, painted a vivid, unbidden picture in my mind's eye. His pruney old mouth pursed on Krista's breasts, her face devoid of the joy that used to light it up, while under the weighty mass of her new husband, inhaling the blended mixture of his cologne, sweat, and onion—an odor she despised.

I lay there, the grating sounds of Haj Mirza Ali Khan's unwelcome ardor ringing in my ears, feeling a deep sense of loss. It was not just the death of my brother but the loss of our dignity.

Krista's soft moans, whether of resignation or disguised distress, were a painful reminder of her decision. It seemed as if with each of his vigorous, thoughtless thrusts, he was not only claiming Krista's body but was also staking a claim on the last vestiges of our family's honor.

In the deep, dark recesses of the night, as Haj Mirza Ali Khan's snores kept me awake, a wave of relentless anger settled within me. It was anger at this interloper's invasion of our lives and the cruel circumstances that had robbed us. But now, Krista was his wife, having traded a piece of her past for a future of protection and financial stability.

The following day, Haj Mirza Ali Khan took a crucial step to ensure Krista's safety by contacting his cousin, revealing his marriage to her, and expressing his concerns about any lingering attention from the Russians.

"I want no trouble with them," he insisted. "What's going on? How can we get them off Krista's tail?"

His cousin, taken aback by the news of Haj Mirza Ali Khan's marriage to a woman young enough to be his daughter and just a couple of days after news of her husband's death, paused before congratulating him.

"Seriously, you married her? I didn't expect this, but congratulations," he said, trying to mask his surprise. "Let me look into it. I'll get back to you on this."

Chapter 28

"In a world of hunters, the wise man learns to run."

Chinese Proverb

As the Allies intensified their hunt for Ravenshadow, in the quiet of his room, he scribbled notes revealing his dire situation: *The walls seem to close in, the once concealed darkness that hid my actions now flicker with the threat of exposure. Alone, trapped in a web of my own making, I find myself at the mercy of a never-ending chase. The solitude is suffocating, a constant reminder of the isolation that has become my only faithful companion.*

Once clear lines between ally and adversary blur, leaving me adrift in a sea of doubt, with nowhere to turn. The ever-present specter of capture looms like a dark cloud over my every move. I feel that I can not stay much longer in this town. The Soviet papers are starting to mention my name. Big photos of me are published all over Iran. The last few days have just been hell.

Being severed from all ties to my homeland for years on end; the utter inability to connect with my family and kin, and those from our race; forced to interact daily with a people whose customs differ from our own; living as an adversary among foes - unyielding foes at that, in a state of perpetual danger every moment of day and night.

While I face betrayal, deceit, and aggression, not to perish gloriously as a soldier fulfilling a noble act but to face the specter of imprisonment that jeopardizes our entire mission and be cast to the executioner like a common felon. All these trials, both big and small, render my existence a cursed fate....

On the night of August 14th, 1943, a thin crescent moon cast only a sliver of light over Tehran's streets. Shrouded in this veil of secrecy, Spencer set out on yet another mission to capture his nemesis, Ravenshadow. After months of patient investigation, a breakthrough came from crucial intelligence provided by the Soviet secret service. Acting on this tip, Spencer uncovered the hiding place of one of the German agents that had parachuted into Iran—and, ultimately, he located Ravenshadow's hideout.

Understanding the importance of capturing the German spy ringmaster, Spencer took it upon himself to apprehend the agent personally. Not wanting informants to alert Ravenshadow of his plans, Spencer was accompanied only by a sergeant from the Field Security Section as he ventured into the lion's den. There was an eerie tension in anticipation of the impending confrontation between hunter and hunted.

Spencer and his partner stealthily navigated the tangled streets of Tehran, where every doorway threatened a potential ambush. The silence only amplified the frantic pounding of their hearts.

Every rustle of leaves in the wind, each creak of a weathered shop sign, sent a jolt of fear through them. The sweltering summer air hung heavy, a suffocating blanket that muffled their hurried breaths.

As they approached an unassuming dwelling on Naderi Street—the reputed hideout of the German spymaster—Spencer felt a surge of adrenaline. The quiet was a deceitful companion; the night was too still.

At the threshold, Spencer's fingers danced across the lock with a finesse forged in the dark arts of espionage.

The click of the tumblers was music to his ears, and the door swung open, inviting them into a pitch-black abyss. They slipped inside.

The house was a cryptic maze, its corridors hinting at hidden dangers. With every step, they delved deeper into the viper's nest, each corner and doorway an unknown.

Ascending the creaking staircase, a peculiar scent teased Spencer's senses—the unmistakable odor of burning paper. Drawn by this clue, he discovered a dimly lit room where figures shifted and swayed in the flickering light of a crackling fire. One, clearly frenzied and focused, fed the flames with what remained of damning evidence.

The room bristled with tension, a silent duel set against the backdrop of a secret war. Spencer's grip tightened on his revolver as the figure lunged for a hidden pistol. Time slowed as Spencer acted with a marksman's precision. The gunshot shattered the silence, a sharp blast in the confined space. The man collapsed—wounded but alive—his dreams of escape crushed by Spencer's unwavering determination.

Among the rescued documents were plans for catastrophic sabotage and lists of treacherous alliances that stretched deep into the heart of the Middle East. The documents were of the utmost import—a treasure trove of intelligence that would tilt the scales of war.

Spencer was able to retrieve the agent's identification, his German gallantry medal - the Iron Cross, maps of Iranian railroads and tunnels ordered destroyed by Adolf Hitler, including a lengthy list of informants, collaborators, and other German agents in the region.

More than 100 Iranian collaborators were arrested based on the discovered documents. Spencer also found pistols, machine guns, grenades, and explosives, in addition to Telefunken radio equipment the agents used to communicate discreetly with Berlin.

Ravenshadow was positively identified as Richard August, alias Franz Mayer, the name Arash had given Russian intelligence in Rasht. Khadeyev had shared this information with British security officials in Tehran, who were hunting the German spy. Spencer's find was not only evidence but also the key to dismantling the Franz Gruppe and foiling a plot that threatened to decimate the Allied leadership.

It was rumored that upon Mayer's capture, the Iron Cross that Spencer found in the German's hideout was presented to Churchill as a gift, considering that the plan was to assassinate the British prime minister and the other two Allied leaders on November 30th, Churchill's 69th birthday.

German World War II Iron Cross, 1939

Mayer's capture was a feat of such significance that the H.M. Minister in Tehran penned a letter of commendation, urging that Spencer's heroic deeds be recognized with a gallantry award. Yet, such was the nature of this clandestine war that the recommendation for Spencer's award came with a caveat—no details of his daring action were to be published in the London Gazette or elsewhere. Secrecy was paramount.

🐈 🐈 🐈

During questioning, Franz, with his arm in a sling from the gunshot, surveyed the makeshift interrogation room with a flicker of amusement dancing in his steely blue eyes.

The Allies yearned to unravel the enigma of the German operation, a feat executed with such brilliance that it had left them floundering in the dark. They wondered how the Germans moved all these materials undetected.

Franz decided to indulge Spencer in a morsel of truth, a tempting appetizer to sate the British ravenous curiosity without divulging the truly sensitive methods German ingenuity had meticulously crafted.

"Theatrics," he rumbled, his voice a low growl, "are often the most effective tool at an illusionist's disposal. Dazzle and distract are the keys."

He leaned forward, his gaze meeting Spencer's.

"You seek the grand secret, the technological marvel that allowed us to move mountains under your very noses? I assure you, there is no such marvel."

A slow, deliberate smile spread across Franz's face. "We employed the oldest, most time-tested method in the book."

Franz chuckled, a dry rasping sound that unnerved the young British officer taking notes. "Ten camels. Ten magnificent beasts of burden, as silent as the desert sands. They carried our little secret from a dusty outpost near Qom after the materials were flown in from Germany by transport plane. We were able to move many things from a place that would likely escape your notice on a map right into the bustling heart of Tehran," he boasted.

Despite their efforts, the British could not extract any useful information from Franz. He had proven to be a master of psychological warfare, maintaining an infuriating composure that rendered traditional interrogation techniques ineffective. His responses were laced with just enough truth to be credible but wrapped in layers of deception that left his interrogators perpetually grasping at straws. The more the British pressed, the more Franz enjoyed the game, his resistance growing.

On what turned out to be Franz's last day of questioning in Tehran, two burly guards came to usher the German out of Spencer's office. A sense of unease twisted in Spencer's gut as Franz hadn't broken under their questioning; no, he'd reveled in it, toying with them.

And Spencer had had enough. It was time to show the German who was in charge as he snapped a single word, "Iraq!"

Franz, a prisoner of war brimming with secrets – was a perfect target for severe interrogation in an unforgiving environment in the deserts of Iraq.

Spencer told Franz that he was being transferred, warning him that the torture that would squeeze every last morsel of information out of him was waiting in the prison camp in Basra.

Hearing that he was to be sent away, Franz's swagger drained.

The man who had been defiant moments earlier stood before Spencer, his shoulders slumping slightly. He spoke, his voice now subdued and devoid of its earlier bravado, a single, unanticipated request cutting through the tension.

"There is one thing," he said. Franz's voice was laced with the desperation of a father's anguish.

"Please," he implored, searching Spencer's face for a trace of compassion. "Let my son, Karl, who lives here in Tehran, know I did not choose to abandon him. He deserves to hear the truth about what has happened and where you are sending me."

The gravity of his request—a father's plea—echoed in the silence that followed. Spencer, whose life had been shaped by the strict demands of duty and the harsh realities of war, now found himself momentarily adrift in the murky waters of moral ambiguity. This request, so profoundly human amidst the dehumanizing espionage and conflict, grated at his conscience.

The silence stretched.

"Your request will be considered," Spencer finally replied, his voice a terse mask hiding the unease Franz's plea had stirred within him. The words, spoken with the finality of command, offered a glimmer of hope but carried the unforgiving nature of war—where promises were as fragile as the lives caught in its crossfire.

In the end, Franz's request remained unfulfilled, and the British didn't tell him that tragedy had already struck with Karl's death.

🐈 🐈 🐈

On September 9, 1943, Iran declared war on Germany. By doing so, Iran sought to facilitate its transition from a state of occupation to one of cooperation with the Allies and to pave the way for membership in the United Nations after the war.

The declaration was also a strategic move to ensure that Iran would be on the winning side of the conflict. It allowed it to have a say in the post-war order and secure the withdrawal of foreign troops from its territory.

Two months later, in November 1943, at the Tehran Conference, the Allies acknowledged Iran's sovereignty and committed to withdrawing troops from Iranian territory six months after the end of the war.

Soviet Premier Joseph Stalin, US President Franklin Delano Roosevelt, and British Prime Minister Winston Churchill (left to right) at the Teheran Conference in 1943.

Chapter 29

"No man, for any considerable period, can wear one face to himself, and another to the multitude, without finally getting bewildered as to which may be the true."

Nathaniel Hawthorne

Basra, Iraq

Upon his arrival at the Basra camp, Franz Mayer was met not with the clanking of prison gates but by the unyielding gaze of two Indian soldiers who led him into the heart of the camp. For the prisoners, each day blended into a numbing routine of roll calls, scant rations, and the relentless, torturous cycle of scorching days and freezing nights.

One sweltering afternoon, Franz stumbled upon a surprising shard of his past. A figure approached him—a thin, bespectacled man with the weary gait of someone well-acquainted with sorrow.

This was Herr Dietrich Vogel, a former teacher at the German school in Tehran where Karl had been a student. The school had been closed by the Allies, with all the male teachers sent to the internment camp in Iraq.

"Herr Mayer?" Vogel's voice trembled slightly as he extended a frail hand, which Franz took, puzzled by the recognition in the man's eyes.

"It is you, isn't it? I was Karl's teacher. I believe I saw you at several school events," as he introduced himself.

Franz, caught off guard, searched his memory and replied, "Yes, yes, of course. How do you find yourself here, Herr Vogel?"

Vogel sighed, his stare drifting momentarily across the barren landscape before returning to Franz.

"Like many, I was caught in the wrong place at the wrong time. A while after the Allied forces took Tehran, they closed our school and rounded up those of us they deemed a threat or of some value for exchange. Despite my protests and lack of political ties, my German heritage was enough to land me here."

The teacher's expression softened as they found shade under a stunted tree, and he smiled wistfully.

"I remember Karl well, a bright and compassionate boy. He was eager to learn and stood up for what was right. I recall once, he defended a classmate who was being bullied because his parents were rumored to be Nazi sympathizers. Karl stepped in and argued against the cruelty with such maturity—it left an impression on all of us."

Franz listened to Herr Vogel's memories of his son, a deep sense of pride swelling within him.

"That sounds like Karl," he said. "He's always had a strong sense of justice, even from a young age. It is one of his great qualities."

But as he savored this moment of pride, Vogel became serious, and the conversation took a heart-stopping turn.

"Herr Mayer," Vogel hesitated, his voice fading into the silence as if the words themselves were painful to utter.

"While we were at the German embassy, waiting for our fate, rumors circulated among the staff… about Karl…"

Franz interrupted him, "What rumors?"

Herr Vogel was surprised Franz seemed unaware. Still, he continued, his voice tinged with hesitation.

"They said Karl... while cleaning his rifle, it accidentally went off, and he was killed. Is it true? If so, I wanted to offer my condolences."

The words struck Franz like a bullet, not unlike the one that had purportedly claimed Karl's life. His vision blurred as a shiver ran through him despite the heat. Franz's face turned pale as he tried to process Vogel's words.

"Karl... dead?" He repeated. "No, no. That can't be true. Karl has handled rifles since he was a boy. He's always been so careful. It just doesn't make sense."

He searched Vogel's face desperately, looking for any sign that this was some twisted joke, a misunderstanding.

"There must be some mistake," Franz insisted, his voice trembling. "Maybe... maybe it was someone else. It can't be Karl. It just can't be."

Franz's thoughts spun in a frantic whirl, and he grasped for any explanation that could make sense of what he had just heard.

"Who told you this? How do you know it was Karl? There must be some confusion. I need to know more... I have to find out the truth." His voice trembled with determination and fear.

Tears welled as the reality of Vogel's words began to sink in, but Franz clung to hope, to denial. Vogel shook his head sadly, "I'm sorry for bringing it up, Herr Mayer. I'm not certain if it's true. I have no further details. That's why I asked; forgive me, it was just something whispered among us."

Franz's mind churned with unanswered questions. His role as a spy had always been about keeping secrets and manipulating truths. Yet here he was, utterly oblivious to what might have happened to his own flesh and blood.

He began to lose his composure, his voice cracking with the weight of his emotions, *How could this have happened?* Franz murmured to himself. He looked back at Vogel, searching for any sign of falsehood, but found only genuine sympathy, a sight that shattered the last remnants of his resolve.

As Vogel futilely patted his shoulder, attempting to offer comfort, Franz felt a hollow emptiness. The world around him—the endless desert, the barbed wire, the distant palm trees—faded into a gray haze.

He was blindsided by the most heart-wrenching news a father could receive, even for someone entangled in a web of espionage. Franz, the spymaster, had no tenderness—he was a man of iron, but even a man of iron melts like wax when his child is stricken down. And now, the Franz of many faces was simply a father grappling with an unspeakable loss; his heart lay bare under the Basra sun.

It felt as if the rigid, unyielding ground beneath Franz's feet began to give way. His son Karl, the boy with the kind heart, the young man who knew how to handle a rifle since he was old enough to hold one—could he truly be gone?

Franz trudged through the parched camp, the harsh wind scouring his skin with sand. The other prisoners, a sea of haggard faces etched with despair, swam before him. Their suffering seemed distant, a muted symphony of coughs and groans barely registering in his numbed mind.

Every face he saw, every snippet of overheard conversation, felt surreal, part of a world to which he no longer entirely belonged. He replayed Vogel's words, each iteration a hammer blow to his spirit: *...They said he died accidentally while cleaning his rifle...*

Franz could no longer bear the uncertainty eating at him. Determined to uncover what happened to his son, he went to the camp administrator's quarters. As he approached, he steeled himself for the conversation ahead, every step feeling heavier with the weight of worry. Franz knew this was his only chance to discover the truth.

At the helm of the British camp, Captain Thornton projected an air of unwavering authority, and those under his command knew him to be a man of principle and fairness.

"Captain Thornton," Franz began, "May I have a word with you?"

Thornton looked up from his desk, assessing Franz curiously.

"Of course, Herr Mayer. What is it?"

Franz took a deep breath, "I need to know the truth about my son, Karl. I was just told by another prisoner, a man who was his teacher in Tehran, that Karl is dead. Tell me, is it true? Spencer promised to tell my son I was in this camp. Do you know if he contacted Karl?"

A flicker of compassion broke through the Captain's usual stern facade.

"Please, have a seat, Herr Mayer."

Franz sat down, his heart pounding as he waited.

Thornton slung back his chair and crossed the room to the imposing file cabinet that lined one wall. He ran a finger down the labels, pulling out a manila folder with frayed edges.

He then settled back into his chair at his desk, the leather creaking beneath him. The Captain opened the folder, the crisp pages rustling as he turned them. His brows furrowed as he absorbed the grim details. After a short while, Thornton closed the folder with a soft thump.

He leaned forward, his hands clasped on the polished surface of his desk.

"Herr Mayer," he began, his voice heavy with sympathy, "I won't lie to you. The reports we've received confirm the heartbreaking news about your son."

He paused, allowing the words to sink in.

"It says Karl Mayer died from a gunshot wound. The official explanation is an accident during rifle maintenance."

The Captain then gently continued, "Your son has been laid to rest in the Polish cemetery in Tehran."

He added, "I'm sorry for your loss."

A lump formed in Franz's throat. "How come no one told me? Did Spencer know? But how can you be sure the information you have is correct? Karl was experienced with firearms. He would not make such a mistake!"

The Captain sighed. "I can't provide any more information as our details are sparse."

Franz's voice trembled in anger. "It just doesn't make sense. So, am I to accept this vague explanation and move on?"

Thornton met his gaze steadily. "I know it is not what you wanted to hear, Herr Mayer. But there is nothing else we can do."

He nodded slowly, a resigned acceptance, as he turned to leave Captain Thornton's office. But then, Franz paused at the doorway and turned back to face the Captain. His eyes burned with an intensity that cut through the thick haze of despair.

"Captain Thornton," he said, his voice steady but edged with a dangerous determination. "If the official channels can't provide me with the answers I need about my son, then I may have to find those answers myself."

Thornton frowned. "What are you suggesting?"

Franz replied defiantly, "Captain, I've lived my life navigating dangers far greater than your prison camp can offer. And speaking of your camp," he added sarcastically, "It's not the fortress you might think it is."

Thornton's face darkened, a mix of concern and anger. "Is that a threat? Are you suggesting escape?"

Franz shrugged nonchalantly. "I'm simply stating that if the truth about my son is beyond the walls of this camp, then so be it. I'll find a way to uncover it myself."

The Captain stepped closer, his voice dropping to a stern warning.

"I don't like your tone! You should choose your words carefully. The consequences of such action would be dire."

But Franz's mind was made up. He stared at Thornton, his demeanor unflinching. The Captain didn't like Franz's attitude and lost his temper, barking, "You are dismissed, Herr Mayer!"

He then called his sergeant, requesting that additional guards be posted and that they monitor Mayer's activities. As Franz left his office, the Captain felt uneasy as he continued to watch him walk away.

As the day bled into the evening, the cold seeped into Franz's bones. He now stood as a sorry figure against endless sand and wire. The spy and strategist Franz Mayer was trapped, not just by the physical confines of his imprisonment, but by the loss of Karl.

After a few weeks in Basra, Franz Mayer was transferred to Egypt for further questioning.

In Alexandria, the sweltering humidity clung to Franz like a second skin. The British interrogation rooms, austere and airless, became his theater of endurance. Days blurred into weeks, each filled with probing questions, veiled threats, and the constant drone of a ceiling fan that did little to dispel the heat. But Franz remained an enigma, his determination growing stronger with each failed attempt to uncover what he so carefully concealed from them.

Unbeknownst to his captors, a shadow play was unfolding beyond the prison walls. A network of German operatives, as silent as desert vipers, was weaving an intricate plan for Franz's extraction. Coded messages, hidden in seemingly innocuous items, were smuggled into the prison. A sympathetic guard, swayed by promises of gold, turned a blind eye to Franz's clandestine preparations.

The night of the escape under the swirling chaos of a sandstorm, Franz, disguised as a British officer, slipped through a hidden passage beneath the prison. The roar of the wind masked the sounds of his escape. A stolen military jeep awaited him, its engine already thrumming, ready to carry him into the tangled alleyways of Alexandria.

Once his escape was discovered, a heart-pounding chase ensued. The jeep weaved through the city's streets, narrowly avoiding British patrols. The storm, though hampering his visibility, also provided the German cover. Franz's pulse hammered in his ears as he navigated towards the rendezvous point, a secluded dock where a small fishing boat, its crew loyal to the Reich, waited to spirit him away.

News of his escape reached London like a shockwave. Enraged and humiliated, the British high command launched a massive manhunt, scouring the Mediterranean for any trace of the elusive spy. But Franz was already gone, vanishing into the vastness of the sea, his destination the neutral shores of Spain.

Rumors rippled through the intelligence community, with some claiming he had been seen in Madrid while others placed him in a remote mountain village. The most compelling tale told of a daring journey across the Pyrenees—a clandestine trek through snow-laden passes to the sanctuary of Switzerland.

Franz Mayer, the ghost who slipped through Britain's fingers, was said to have resurfaced in the heart of Europe. This tale only added to his enigmatic legacy.

Some even suggested that the British considered recapturing Franz and turning him into a double agent against the Soviets. The thought was dismissed, bolstered by insights from Spencer, who argued Mayer's allegiance would never sway. His heart was tethered to the Fatherland's call.

Chapter 30

*"...When you come out of the storm,
you won't be the same person who walked in.
That's what this storm's all about."*

Haruki Murakami

Haj Mirza Ali Khan and Krista had tied the knot in a sudden strategic marriage out of necessity. Haj Mirza Ali Khan's cousin delivered the best wedding present for the couple when he called to report that the German spy Franz Mayer had been caught. He mentioned that the Russians wouldn't pursue them, given that the British were now involved and the spy network disbanded.

Krista had asked her husband to find out if they were going to send Arash's body to Tehran for a proper burial. He asked, but the cousin replied, "They've buried him, and no one knows where. No need to open old wounds. Go enjoy your honeymoon with your young wife."

That was the answer he wanted to hear.

And life trudged on even with the constant tramp of Allied boots on the streets of Tehran. Krista navigated her role as Haj Mirza Ali Khan's wife with quiet resilience. Though she had arrived a stranger, Krista now established a place for herself in her new country.

The days were filled with the mundane tasks of managing a household, punctuated by the occasional dinner where Haj Mirza Ali Khan entertained guests from the bazaar, foreign businessmen, and military officials, reflecting the shifting alliances and economic opportunities from the war.

As Haj Mirza Ali Khan's influence grew, I still harbored mixed feelings about our new family dynamic. I was caught between my past and present, even though I understood what Krista had told me: survival in such tumultuous times often requires hard choices and unlikely alliances. Still, the unease between me and Haj Mirza Ali Khan was undeniable. Despite Krista's pleas for civility, my interactions with him remained superficial, masking a deep loathing. I couldn't shake the feeling that something about him was profoundly unsettling despite his role in saving us from doom.

Haj Mirza Ali Khan's presence was a constant undercurrent, a jarring interruption in the familiar melody of our family life. And he had a terrible habit that made me miserable. He loved to smoke.

There was no pause, no break between cigarettes for Haj Mirza Ali Khan. He was a human chimney. He'd barely finish a stick before a fresh one was already lit, the ember of the last still glowing in the ashtray.

Cigarettes perpetually clung to his lips, burning down at an alarming rate. Smoke billowed from him in dense grey plumes, obscuring his face and turning every room into a hazy fog.

And if an ashtray wasn't within arm's reach, smoldering butts found their way anywhere – disposed of with a nonchalant flick of the wrist into unsuspecting planters, sometimes blackening the leaves with a defiant sizzle.

The acrid tang permeated everything. The odor clung to the furniture and curtains like a stubborn guest. Even my clothes reeked as I was unable to escape the stench. And it wasn't just his smoking. Like a slow, creeping vine, it had begun to entangle Krista, too.

She used to light a cigarette during social gatherings, sharing a wisp of smoke with friends on the balcony. However, her occasional puffs had become frequent under her new husband's influence. I'd catch her, a cigarette dangling from her fingers, mirroring his unconscious inhales and exhales. The once vibrant scent of her perfume was now tinged with the overpowering smell of tobacco.

The house itself became a monument to their shared habit. Ashtrays became graveyards of extinguished cigarettes, overflowing with spent filters. Even open windows offered little escape, the stubborn fumes curling back in with the breeze, refusing to be banished.

In addition to this annoying habit, Haj Mirza Ali Khan also turned out to be an insecure man with an insatiable hunger for approval from others. His craving for recognition overshadowed everything else, which was pathetic and grating.

He desired to project an image of belonging to a world that barely recognized him. Krista's effortless connections to foreign guests made her his passport to that world. The soirees she hosted, a symphony of laughter and clinking crystal, were his glittering stage.

I saw through each forced laugh, boastful story, and attempt to dominate the conversation. It was a transparent act, a desperate yearning for a spotlight that never found Haj Mirza Ali Khan.

Aware of my feelings toward him, he tried to bridge the gap between us. But each time he addressed me with *pesaram*, the Persian term for 'my son,' it annoyed me. I was not his son, and he was nothing like the man my father was. So, his attempts at closeness only unsettled me more.

One day, shortly before I was to graduate, Haj Mirza Ali Khan engaged me in conversation, sharing stories from his youth.

"Pesaram," he began, with nostalgia in his voice, "As I've already told you and Krista, I was sent to Germany for my studies as a teenager but had to return hastily upon my father's death. One of my greatest regrets is that I never finished my education."

Then, he made a surprising suggestion.

"Europe is in ruins now," he continued, "but you should study in America when the war ends. America is untouched, a land of opportunity. Your father, may he rest in peace; he wanted you to study there. This war has taken much from us but shouldn't steal your future."

At first, I suspected a ruse. The mansion was partly my inheritance, and I was worried he wanted to usurp it if I was out of the way. But then, as if he had read my mind, he added, "Your inheritance will be taken care of. I propose to buy your share at a fair price. I can invest the rest for you until you return. And as my gift to you, pesaram, I want to pay for your education in America."

He then delved into his recent ventures, speaking proudly of his business savvy.

"With the Americans now part of the Allied efforts here, I've started working with them. Before the war came to Iran, I took a huge risk, bought thousands of tires, and stored them away. Fortunately, the gamble paid off. With the American military's dire need for truck tires, I'm making a substantial profit selling to them."

He leaned in, "And Sohrab, the good news is, as a result, I have a contact at the American Embassy. He said he would help get you a visa to study in America."

Maybe he wanted to get me out of his and Krista's lives, and this was the best way to do it, but I didn't care what his reasons were. This generous proposition began to soften the hard edges of my resentment. Perhaps my grudge was more about Haj Mirza Ali Khan having replaced Arash than anything else.

His offer to support my education in America was disarming despite our differences. It forced me to acknowledge a side of him I hadn't considered before — one capable of generosity and forward-thinking. This gesture showed a level of care and investment in my future that I hadn't expected.

Undoubtedly, my newfound perspective was colored by my eagerness to go to America. Escaping the stifling atmosphere of our household and the chance to start anew in a land of opportunity was alluring, making it easier for me to view him less harshly. It was a moment of conflicting emotions, where gratitude and skepticism coexisted, leaving me uncertain about how to reconcile my feelings toward Haj Mirza Ali Khan.

Chapter 31

"Saying nothing… sometimes says the most."
Emily Dickinson

It was just a little while after their marriage when Krista's condition became apparent, stirring a question in my mind. The news of her pregnancy seemed oddly timed.

At his age, Haj Mirza Ali Khan was overjoyed at the prospect of fatherhood. He paraded Krista's swelling belly before guests with a pride that bordered on conquest - a grand achievement akin to scaling the highest mountain or unearthing a long-buried treasure. Krista, too, was ecstatic that her fears of barrenness had finally been vanquished with this blessing.

About seven months later, the child, born prematurely–*haft-maheh* in Persian– arrived in a world of rumors and sideways glances. Despite his early arrival, the boy was surprisingly robust, and his health was a small miracle.

Krista named the boy *Omid*, the Persian word for hope. In him, she found fulfillment in her deepest yearnings. For her, the child was a beacon of hope in the bleakness of war.

Yet, beneath the surface of joy and pride lay an untold truth. Omid, with his fair skin and blond hair, bore no resemblance to Haj Mirza Ali Khan. Instead, as time passed, a striking likeness to Karl became evident.

The evening of Franz's visit to Krista's study flashed back in my memory. When Krista had appeared slightly disheveled, her hurried explanation sounded inconsequential. But now, it hung there, a silent witness to a secret rendezvous.

Haj Mirza Ali Khan, blissfully unaware, would hold the child aloft, proudly showing off his heir to the guests, remarking on the boy's fair features with the phrase, *"Meebeeni che booreh, be khanevadeyeh Krista rafteh."* (Do you see how blond he is? He takes after Krista's family).

Krista, for her part, skirted around the subject, her joy in motherhood overshadowing the hidden truth.

A while after Omid was born, Krista asked, "Sohrab, would you like to hold him?"

Omid, impossibly small and wrapped in a pale blue blanket, seemed fragile in her arms. A pang of nervousness shot through me, and I thought, *What if I drop him?*

Taking a deep breath, I reached out, my hands hesitant at first, then slowly enveloping Omid. He was a picture of innocence. His eyes, still unfocused, fluttered shut as his tiny hand instinctively grasped my finger. An unbidden love bloomed in my chest for this sweet child.

However, hidden within my love for him, I was also convinced Franz was his father, responsible for the gaping hole in our lives. This truth choked me; I could never voice my true feelings to Krista, not when she looked at her son with such tenderness.

But Omid was innocent—a blank slate untouched by his father's sins, no more deserving of blame than poor Karl, who shouldered the punishment of that same father's transgressions. It was a suffocating secret—this affection warring with a quiet simmering anger. Omid was a beautiful bud blossoming in the world, but with the thorns of his bloodline, I couldn't ignore it.

Krista's love for the child was pure, untainted by the darkness of his true lineage – the son of a Nazi spy, a man whose activities had led to her own husband's untimely death. As the child grew, so did the unspoken understanding between Krista and me. We never broached the topic of her secret tethering to Franz.

After Omid's birth, Krista's relationship with Haj Mirza Ali Khan grew stronger. His fluency in German became an advantage, and she decided they should speak only German at home so that Omid could grow up bilingual in Persian and German.

This decision mirrored how, when Krista first arrived in Iran, she had asked Arash to speak only Persian until she could learn the language. Their shared love for the child bridged the gaps of their hastily arranged marriage, creating a bond that, while fragile, was genuine in its affection and care.

🐈 🐈 🐈

Throughout the war, our home had been a place where fear and death lingered like unwanted guests, seeping into its walls and dimming its once-vibrant spirit. But with the arrival of little Omid, a flicker of joy pierced through the subdued mood that had hung over the house. Omid's presence brought a much-needed brightness into our lives. His playful antics and curious nature filled our home with a warmth that had been absent for far too long. Omid was a sign that life could blossom anew in a house that had known so much sorrow.

With Omid's arrival, Krista hired a nanny for the child, a beautiful Polish woman named Gabriela, who came to live with us. She was in her mid-twenties with an indomitable spirit, having survived savage treatment by the Soviets.

Born into a modest Catholic family in Warsaw, Gabriela's life was upended when the iron grip of Stalin's regime ensnared Poland. Her father, a professor of philosophy at the University of Warsaw, and her mother, a renowned pianist, were considered members of the intelligentsia and seen as threats to Soviet control.

In the dead of night, Gabriela's family was shattered as they were forcibly taken from their home and deported to the icy wastelands of Siberia. The Russians used these deportations to remote areas as a strategy to weaken the Polish state's foundation and prevent any organized resistance.

Later in the war, there was growing international pressure from Britain and the United States for the Soviet Union to improve its treatment of Polish citizens. Poland was heavily ravaged by war, where cities were destroyed, and the country was under Nazi occupation in the west and Soviet control in the east. Therefore, returning to a homeland that was in the midst of conflict and destruction was incredibly dangerous and uncertain.

So to bolster his partnership with the Allies in the war effort against Nazi Germany, Stalin released the Polish refugees and allowed them to come to Iran, where the British and Americans had a presence.

This relocation of refugees to Iran also alleviated the strain on Soviet resources while maintaining Stalin's alliance with the Western powers. Upon their release, about 2,500 Polish citizens arrived in Iran each day, totaling more than 100,000, with nearly 5,000 of them Jewish.

Polish refugees evacuated from the Soviet Union to Iran in 1942

The severity of the labor camps was a crucible, forging Gabriela into a woman of strength and resolve. Her parents had died in Siberia, succumbing to the grueling conditions in the cold from starvation and disease.

Gabriela and her younger brother, Aleksy, made the arduous journey ferried across the Caspian to the shores of northern Iran. They were broken, sick, and hungry. Within days of their arrival at the Iranian port of Pahlavi, Aleksy died of pneumonia and was buried there.

Gabriela's new life began on a bus to a refugee camp for Poles in Tehran. There, she found herself in a land vastly different from the plains of Siberia. One Sunday soon after that, fate intertwined her path with Krista's in a Tehran church. Krista saw a kindred spirit in Gabriela, with both women seeking comfort in their shared European heritage.

When Gabriela entered our lives, I was immediately captivated by her. I had never been close to a woman her age to whom I felt such a strong attraction. The ordinary world seemed to fade when she was around, replaced by a spark of something new and exciting. I found myself seeking her out more and more, hungry for that feeling. Every smile she sent my way felt precious. We often spent time together while she looked after Omid, as I always managed to find an excuse to be near her and available.

Once, while Gabriela was sitting quietly in the nursery with Omid, I joined her. The room was unnervingly silent, unlike the emotions flickering across her face, as she was seemingly consumed in her thoughts.

I wanted to know more about what had happened to her before coming to Iran, and this seemed like the perfect moment to ask her.

Gabriela told me that being in Iran felt like heaven compared to the hell of Siberia.

"When we reached Iran, everything was beautiful and welcoming. Persians greeted us with warm smiles. Even the Indian soldiers looked at us with pity.

"You know, the instant I got off the boat in Pahlavi, I fell to the sand on the beach and kissed it as others sat on the shore, praying and weeping. The ships were overcrowded, with passengers covered in rags and lice. They looked like walking skeletons.

"After several days in quarantine in a warehouse near the port, we were sent to Tehran. As we traveled through the small towns on our way, Persian children threw things at us, which terrified us."

I got upset hearing that, and noticing the look on my face, she quickly clarified, "We thought they were throwing stones at us, but we soon found out they were throwing apples and candies. When we got to Tehran, we were captivated. Everything felt magical and unreal."

I sensed that Gabriela carried the heavy burden of being her family's sole survivor. She was reluctant to revisit "the bad times" by recounting her family's harrowing struggles in Russia. Instead, she preferred to speak only of her good memories of life in Poland and the beauty of her homeland.

But I was curious about how she left Poland and got to Siberia, and I pressed on. After some time, Gabriela finally relented and began to tell me.

"It was always in the dead of night, Sohrab," she began, her thoughts drifting back in time.

"The NKVD (the Soviet police) would come without warning. There was just a loud knock on the door, and that was it. You had only a few minutes to pack, to grab whatever you could. Families were torn from their beds, from their lives, without even knowing where they were being taken or if they would ever return."

Her hand gently stroked Omid's back, soothing the baby with her touch while I listened to her story.

"When they came for us, they took us and loaded us onto trains like cattle, cramped and cold. No one told us anything. People were scared and confused. Many lost everything in those moments. The trek was long and torturous, a nightmare with no end."

She paused, her words catching in her throat as if the memories were fresh.

"But in all that darkness, there was light. Before leaving our home, the authorities let us quickly gather a few personal items. My father smuggled a book he used to teach his university students. When my mother complained that he should make room for more necessary items, he said this book was his most important possession."

I asked, "What kind of book?"

Gabriela said, "It was by an American philosopher, Thoreau. On that long train ride to Siberia, my father read to us from it. His voice, steady and sure, would cut through the stench and the despair, reminding us of something bigger than our suffering."

Gabriela's voice grew firmer, reflecting the strength she drew from these memories; "Thoreau said, '*However mean your life is, meet it and live it; do not shun it and call it hard names. It is not so bad as you think. The fault-finder will find faults even in paradise. Love your life, difficult as it is...You must live in the present, launch yourself on every wave, find your eternity in each moment...*' Those words... they were my salvation. Even in that horrid place, we learned to find moments of peace and cherish the small kindnesses we could offer one another."

I was absorbed in her story. I had so many questions. "What happened when you got to Siberia?"

Looking down at Omid, she sighed, "When we arrived at the camp, the Russian commandant told the prisoners that we would remain there forever. There were no fences to keep us in. If we ran into the forest, we would get eaten by wolves. Many did try to get out through the forest, but we never saw them again. There was nowhere to go.

"My father told us that Thoreau said, '*Fools stand on their island of opportunities and look toward another land.*' At first, I was like one of those fools, longing for a home that was no longer mine, dreaming of a place that didn't exist anymore."

I didn't understand what she meant; why did she consider herself a fool for wanting to have back the life she had lost. Gabriela could sense my confusion. She lifted her head, and her eyes met mine.

"There were some who couldn't endure it, so desperate they wanted to kill themselves. The fear of not knowing what would happen next was a slow, creeping death—a crushing suffocation of hopelessness. But then,

I realized something. My father probably knew there was no going back.

"He understood there was no return to our former lives, no distant shores to pin our dreams on. Perhaps that's why he incessantly read Thoreau to us—to find our eternity in each moment."

She paused to let her words sink in, then continued, "I chose to embrace my destiny, to find my own eternity there, even in those sordid conditions. Then, one day, after so much suffering, they dragged us down to the river, and we thought of the horrible things they were going to do to us. But instead, told us we were free."

She held Omid closer, and her expression softened. Despite her adversity—a journey marked by loss and survival—she had an unyielding spirit. But I could also see how the loss of her family haunted her. She carried a locket around her neck, in which she had squeezed their pictures. Whenever Gabriela spoke of her family, her fingers instinctively clutched the locket, tenderly caressing it and pressing it firmly into her palm as though embracing them.

The deaths of Arash and Haidar, both caught in the ruthless gears of war, had left a void in me filled with grief and unresolved anger. But I sensed a subtle shift within me as Gabriela's tale offered me a different perspective to understand my family's pain.

It was true—I was not alone in my grief, nor were we as a people unique in our suffering. She had faced losses yet carried herself with quiet strength, continuing to find reasons to embrace life, even one marred by tragedy. I realized how wrong I was, selfishly thinking that my troubles were the heaviest.

Gabriela opened up new worlds to me. I felt something beyond admiration, a pull I couldn't understand.

Was it love? I wondered. It was probably lust. Whatever it was, I wanted it badly.

My thoughts were a tangled mess, emotions swirling within me like a storm. Everything seemed to fall into place whenever I was with Gabriela. My heart raced at the thought of her. This burgeoning feeling was a secret I kept from everyone, even from her.

One evening, as the sun set and a cool breeze offered relief from the day's intense heat, Gabriela sat by the ornamental pool, resting after Omid had finally fallen asleep. I joined her, and we decided to cool our feet in the water. We slipped off our shoes, and as Gabriela dipped her feet into the pool, I couldn't help but notice her left foot.

Two of her toes were missing.

It was a surprising contrast to her otherwise graceful appearance. The sight jolted me, a sudden and startling revelation. A brief flicker of discomfort crossed her face as she noticed me staring at her foot.

I had often seen Gabriela favoring her left foot slightly when she walked. Still, out of respect for her, I had never asked about the gentle limp. That night, however, curiosity found its way into our tranquil setting.

"Does it bother you?" she asked softly, pointing to her foot, seemingly vulnerable.

Of course, it bothered me, but I quickly composed myself.

"No, Gabriela, not at all. I just… I didn't know."

She smiled faintly, "It's a part of my story, Sohrab. A chapter that was written in Siberia."

I nodded, but the question hovered between us. Gabriela hid her foot beneath the water's surface before slowly telling me what had happened.

"During the winter in Siberia, I was forced to work outside in the freezing cold. One day, the temperature dropped so low that I lost all feeling in my feet."

She paused, her voice tinged with the memory.

"By the time morning came, the damage was done. The frostbite was severe on my left foot. The camp authorities, crude and indifferent as they were, performed a rudimentary amputation. They had no medicine or sedatives. I was given a piece of leather to bite down on, and they cut off my frostbitten toes with a small saw."

I shuddered at the thought, horrified by what she went through.

"Gabriela, that's unimaginable. How did you endure it?"

She looked at me, her expression mirroring her resilience. "The suffering was overwhelming, but you endure because you have no choice. Pain becomes a part of you, something you learn to live with."

Gabriela turned her gaze back to the shimmering water, her fingers touching the water's surface, and said, "There was a woman in the camp, an old healer who lost her whole family. She said that scars were not just marks of hardship but badges of honor. She told me, 'Wear your scars with pride, for they are the stories of your strength.'"

From that day forward, my admiration for Gabriela only grew. Her limp was not merely a mark of past suffering but a testament to her unyielding determination to survive.

The following afternoon, when Gabriela was picking flowers in the garden, I approached her with my father's worn leather diary and the pretext of nostalgia.

"Gabriela," I began, my voice unsteady, "may I share something with you? It's from my father's diary."

"Of course, Sohrab," she replied, wiping her hands on her apron and sitting on the nearby bench.

I sat beside her, the diary on my lap, its pages fluttering in the breeze.

"My father loved Persian poetry, and he recorded a poem by Hafez," I explained. I think it's beautiful."

I opened the diary to the marked page, my fingers tracing the lines of the poet's words that my father had inscribed years ago. I read aloud, my voice stilted at first but growing more confident with each word:

> "Hast thou forgotten when thy stolen glance, Was turned to me, when on my happy face
> Clearly thy love was writ, which doth enhance, All happiness? or when my sore disgrace
> (Hast thou forgot?) drew from thine eyes reproof, And made thee hold thy sweet red lips aloof,
> Dowered, like Jesus' breath, with healing grace?"

As I read, the world seemed to narrow down to the bench where we sat. I dared to glance at Gabriela, and with her eyes fixed on me, a gentle understanding dawned in them:

> "The goblet's carbuncle (hast thou forgot?),
> Laughed out aloud, and speech flew hot, And fast between thy ruby lips and mine!
> Hast thou forgotten when thy cheek's dear torch, Lighted the beacon of desire in me,
> And when my heart, like foolish moths that scorch, Their wings and yet return, turned all to thee?"

As I finished the poem, my voice trailed off into the stillness of the garden. The unnerving silence that followed seemed to stretch on endlessly. With my heart racing, I closed the diary.

"That was beautiful. Your father must have been very affectionate," Gabriela softly shared.

"Yes, he was," I agreed, searching her face for a sign, a hint that she understood the poem was more than just a recitation, that it was the mirror of my heart's yearning.

But I said nothing more, maintaining ambiguity for fear of direct rejection, letting the poem linger between us, my confession hidden within the verses of Hafez, whispered to the garden winds.

"Sohrab," Gabriela's voice drew me back, creating an air of expectancy.

"You mean a lot to me…" she began, her words trailing off as if dancing around a delicate truth. I leaned in, my anticipation building, searching her face for signs of the confession I longed to hear, teasing the edges of my heart with possibilities.

Finally, Gabriela said, "I do love you, Sohrab… " with a tenderness that resonated with my deepest desires. However, the undercurrent of her sentiments shifted as she spoke, revealing the true nature of her affection.

"…Like a brother, you remind me of my Aleksy."

She reached out, her hand touching mine, a gesture full of warmth but undeniably platonic. Her words hit like a cold wave. I didn't want to be loved like a brother, and I especially didn't want to hear it when I sensed a glimmer of what could have been.

Gabriela's revelation shattered my illusions, replacing the dream of romance I had envisioned with the simple truth of brotherly love. This quiet moment of acceptance carried its sting; it was a silent goodbye to a love that would never be.

Part III: The Post-War Years

Chapter 32

"War is a contagion. But like all contagions, it has an end."
Barbara W. Tuchman

Tehran, 1945

The war ended, and a Tehran, once caught in the crosshairs of foreign powers and steeped in uncertainty, was now infused with guarded optimism.

With the cessation of hostilities, plans were made to repatriate the remaining German citizens. It was a complex process, fraught with the logistics of transporting individuals across a war-torn world and the emotional burden of uprooted lives. The German settlers, returning to a homeland ravaged by war, had to face the harsh realities of rebuilding their lives from the ashes. Meanwhile, we Iranians felt excited, knowing that the foreign occupiers marching through our streets would soon leave.

Their departure would mean more than empty barracks; it would leave Iran grappling with its newfound freedom and the scars of occupation. The Allied victory stirred mixed feelings among us. Some breathed sighs of relief, anticipating a return to normalcy, while others, tempered by unfulfilled promises, remained skeptical.

Some secretly had longed for a German triumph, hoping for a reprieve from the grip of British and Soviet influence. The occupation fostered deep resentment among the people due to the immense suffering they endured, the food shortages, inflation, and the forced abdication of our king.

People reverently spoke of Reza Shah, admiring his leadership and accomplishments, though there was an underlying sense of betrayal. They mourned the loss of a patriotic leader who had modernized Iran, only to be ousted by foreign powers serving their own interests.

Distant celebrations marked the war's end, but Tehran's mood was one of reflective quietude, not joy. Our nation was oscillating between relief and unease, unsure of the future. Would all the foreign soldiers depart, or would Iran remain a pawn in their strategic games?

This period signaled a new beginning for me. I realized that we Iranians deserved to be the architects of our future, not mere onlookers, fully aware that the road ahead would be challenging. The possibility of studying in the United States gave me hope – America was a place where I could gain the education and skills necessary to return and serve my country in its quest for an independent and prosperous future.

Yet, I couldn't shake the doubts lingering in my mind. Who knew how long I would be away in America? Once someone sets foot in such a place, the allure of opportunity might make it difficult to leave. Even the most noble intentions can falter in the face of comfort and the promises of a new world.

But before I could embrace this future, I had to confront the ghosts of my past. Something unresolved still tugged at me. In the chaos of those final days, we never found out where Karl was buried. Hoping to pay my respects and find peace, I turned to the well-connected Haj Mirza Ali Khan, who began his inquiries.

He soon learned that, in the days after Karl's death, no one came to claim his body from the morgue.

"Because the authorities couldn't locate his father," Haj Mirza Ali Khan explained, "they buried the German boy with other Christians in Tehran's Polish Cemetery."

The thought of Karl lying unclaimed, abandoned in death, was a heartbreaking reminder that final farewells are a luxury few can afford in wartime.

The Polish Cemetery, Tehran

The cemetery was where thousands of Polish refugees from Siberia who had come to Iran during the war were buried. The tombs of those unidentified held only simple inscriptions, often just numbers and dates, haunting remnants of the anonymous suffering and displacement endured by so many innocents.

I went to the Polish cemetery to visit Karl. Although Gabriela offered to join me, I chose to go alone. Like the

Polish refugees resting there, Karl was also buried far from his homeland. Although his life had been snatched away earlier than it should have been, the difference was that Karl had a choice, while the poor souls in the dirt beside him didn't. And his choice had been a terrible one. Karl's sensitive soul felt the weight of sins, not his own, leading to his desperate escape from reality.

I continued to wrestle with why he did it. I was angry at him for not being stronger. Karl's decision confused me, especially when everyone around us was locked in a daily struggle for survival, fighting against the odds. Instead, he had selfishly chosen to end his own life, consumed by the darkness he saw in his own blood.

Standing before his grave, the cool marble of his tombstone etched with a sole cross, I was flooded with memories. I recalled the long evenings spent tangled in dreams, conversations that offered a haven from the war's incessant clamor.

The cemetery was silent, save for the rustle of leaves and the distant hum of the city. I kneeled close to him and placed my hand on the cold ground, imagining it as a bridge connecting me to Karl.

"My brother from another land," I mumbled, "At least you'll be happy to know that Hitler lost. I know you find some peace in the defeat of the Nazis and their ideology that cast a shadow over your final days. Our friendship was a rare flower that bloomed in this desert land."

In that quiet moment, a sudden memory flashed before me—I recalled Karl's faltering words the day he handed me his uncle's wristwatch. Now, at his gravesite, I understood the foresight behind his gift. Karl had never intended to ask for the watch back; he had known there wouldn't be a return. The day we went to the bathhouse, his misfired joke about leaving me his watch in his will was no joke. And that day, amidst the heartache of what his mother's letter had revealed, I realized I had overlooked the signs of his impending decision.

The truth struck me with a staggering force, and as I felt the steady ticking of the watch against my skin, it became a poignant reminder of a friend lost too soon. Karl had entrusted me with the last remnant of a forsaken heritage, perhaps as his way of making peace with a burdensome legacy.

The silence of the graveyard wrapped around me. Surrounded by all the dead, my thoughts drifted to Arash and Haidar, whose lives had become entangled with Karl's father. The injustice that Arash suffered, being detained and ultimately murdered by the Soviets, and Haidar's untimely death, both due to their association with Franz, kindled a fierce anger within me.

Despite his tragic end, a sobering truth settled in: Karl had a memorial, a piece of earth acknowledging his existence. But Arash and Haidar were denied even this small dignity, their final resting places unknown. Who knew in what dirt pile the Russians had dumped their bodies? There would be no gravesite at which to visit with them; their remains were lost to the anonymity of death's embrace.

In my sorrow, I vowed to visit another graveyard, hoping it would be soon. I prayed that one day I could see Franz's resting place and dance on top of his grave, a joyful dance that the world had finally rid itself of him.

Even though Krista's words from her Bible about forgiveness rang in my ear, this noble sentiment, so righteous on paper, seemed an elusive grace. Forgiveness was a formidable hurdle for me, faced with the scars of betrayal and loss.

I muttered my farewell to Karl. "Your father's actions ripped through our lives like a storm, leaving a trail of destruction. Your father turned out to be the monster you thought he was…"

And I wanted to say more to him, but I couldn't. With a final, lingering look, I got up and walked away. The solitude of the cemetery carried my unvoiced thoughts for Karl and my silent lament for Arash and Haidar, leaving them to settle like dust on Karl's grave.

CHAPTER 33

"Only the dead have seen the end of war."
George Santayana

Tehran, 1946

When the war ended, we were hopeful that the prolonged strain of foreign troops treading our soil was finally over. Talk of independence spread like wildfire. We imagined a future where we Iranians were masters of our fate, liberated from the Allied occupation. But unfortunately, our optimism was short-lived.

While the British and American forces began withdrawing from Iran as agreed at the Tehran Conference, the Soviets entrenched themselves further, seemingly unmovable. Their presence in northern Iran expanded, with more troops and tanks rolling in under the guise of "security measures."

It became painfully clear that what we had envisioned as liberation was only a shift in control. Under the pretext of protecting their interests, the Soviets positioned themselves as the new overseers of our destiny.

The Soviet Union's reluctance to withdraw its troops from Iranian territory, as agreed at the Tehran Conference, further complicated our country's post-war situation. The Russian grasp on Iran was a calculated play in the grand chessboard of global power. With eyes set on the Middle East, Stalin viewed Iran as a pawn to be maneuvered in his quest to checkmate Western influence there.

This Soviet strategy was not only territorial but also economic. The Russians sought to tether this vein to their heartland, dreaming of oil concessions to fuel their empire's expansion and secure its energy future.

Our jubilation at victory quickly soured in the face of this new reality, and the celebrations felt hollow as new challenges emerged. Conversations in the bazaars and tea houses grew tense, with people anxiously debating our next move.

The promise of self-governance slipped further away each day that the Soviet flag flew over our lands in the north. The lingering Red Army presence emboldened and encouraged separatist sentiments among Iran's ethnic minorities, who had long chafed under government policies of cultural and political marginalization. The Soviets actively backed these autonomy movements, seeking to shape them into entities that would ultimately advance Moscow's strategic goals.

I remembered the curious caricature that hung in my father's study years ago, *"The Harmless Necessary Cat,"* where, with forced camaraderie, the British Lion and the Russian Bear discussed how to share Iran. However, with the recent Soviet shenanigans, it was clear that the bear desired to claim the entire country, unshared and wholly conquered.

🐱🐱🐱

As for Commissar Khadeyev, he received a commendation from Stalin, recognizing his role in identifying the notorious Nazi spymaster Mayer. This information ultimately led to Mayer's capture by the

British and derailed the plot to assassinate the Allied leaders. This accolade bolstered Khadeyev's reputation within the Soviet military and intelligence community, reinforcing his position as an essential player in Stalin's plans for the region.

Khadeyev was also personally involved in aiding the separatist movements in northern Iran, particularly the Democratic Party of Azerbaijan and the Kurdish Republic of Mahabad.

His brutal tactics and absolute loyalty to Stalin's directives made him a loathed figure among Iranians. He undertook numerous daring clandestine operations, ruthlessly suppressing opposition and ensuring that pro-Soviet sentiments dominated the local political landscape.

The Commissar cunningly manipulated local leaders and forged alliances with influential tribal chiefs, utilizing propaganda to sow discord among Iranian factions. His efforts were marked by a series of calculated moves, including the deployment of Soviet advisors and the provision of military support to separatist militias.

But Khadeyev's time in the spotlight was brief.

A grave miscalculation involving the local resistance precipitated the Commissar's downfall. Eager to demonstrate his effectiveness, Khadeyev ordered a crackdown on a suspected insurgent stronghold in an upscale residential neighborhood where many government officials lived.

Without the Kremlin's authorization, he carried out the mission with overwhelming force, resulting in significant civilian casualties and widespread destruction. Khadeyev reported the mission as a success, highlighting the elimination of key resistance leaders.

Unbeknownst to the Commissar, several individuals killed in the raid were prominent pro-Soviet figures and covert allies of Moscow. The loss of these assets was a severe blow and a major embarrassment for the Soviet leadership, which enraged Stalin when he found out.

Khadeyev's reckless use of force and failure to correctly identify targets were seen as gross negligence. The incident not only jeopardized Soviet activities but also risked turning local sentiment against the Russians at a crucial juncture.

These Soviet actions in northern Iran led to the Iran crisis of 1946, one of the first confrontations of the Cold War. After significant international pressure and internal political maneuvering, the Soviet forces finally exited Iranian territories in May under the weighty gaze of a world reshaped by conflict.

Upon his return to the Soviet Union, Khadeyev, who dreamt of coming back as a war hero, found his fortunes taking a dramatic downturn. Abandoned by the regime he served, he was stripped of his command and power and relegated to a minor bureaucratic role. His fall from grace was swift and unforgiving, mirroring the fate of many who served Stalin with blind obedience. The regime he had once championed now viewed him as a relic of wartime necessity. Khadeyev faded into obscurity, his once-feared name becoming a mere footnote within the archives of Soviet history.

Chapter 34

"Exile is strangely compelling to think about but terrible to experience. It is the unhealable rift forced between a human being and a native place, between the self and its true home: its essential sadness can never be surmounted."

Edward Said

In 1947, I embarked on a trip that changed the direction of my life. I left behind my home and the familiar streets of Tehran with my sights set on Beirut, Lebanon, the first leg of my travels to America.

On the eve of my departure, Gabriela sought me out, solemnly determined in her stride. She cradled a small, intricately carved amber charm. Gabriela told me this parting gift was known as "Baltic gold," as amber was prized in her country for protection and perseverance.

"In Poland, we believe amber holds the light of the setting sun, a beacon for those who traverse unknown paths," she said softly, a fragile thread in the quiet of my room, with the weight of farewells hanging between us.

"Sohrab," she continued, "This amber has seen the world, from the Baltic shores to the heart of Persia. Let it remind you that no matter how far you go, the light of home is with you."

Then, to my surprise, she asked, "Hast thou forgot?"

I said, "Forgot what?"

She began reciting a line from the poem by Hafez I had read to her one day:

"....All happiness? Or when my sore disgrace
(Hast thou forgot?) drew from thine eyes reproof,
And made thee hold thy sweet red lips aloof...!"

She asked, "Do you remember the day you read this to me?"

The moment stretched; the tension seemed filled with promise. Then Gabriela leaned forward, and her lips met mine in a farewell kiss. It was a kiss tinged with the bitter sorrow of parting. It spoke of possibilities, of what could have been.

That kiss, my first, was a revelation, unlocking a flood of emotions I had never felt before. It was a silent confession that what we shared had grown into something deeper than friendship.

Gabriela stepped back, the amber charm in my hand, and suddenly, the thought of leaving didn't seem as exciting anymore. My first kiss and the gifted charm conspired to anchor me to Tehran, even as my dreams pulled me across the ocean. But, it was a momentary fantasy. I had to go.

Haj Mirza Ali Khan had gone to great lengths to arrange my travel. Most importantly, with the help of his contact at the U.S. Embassy in Tehran, they pulled some strings, and I was admitted to New York University in the fall.

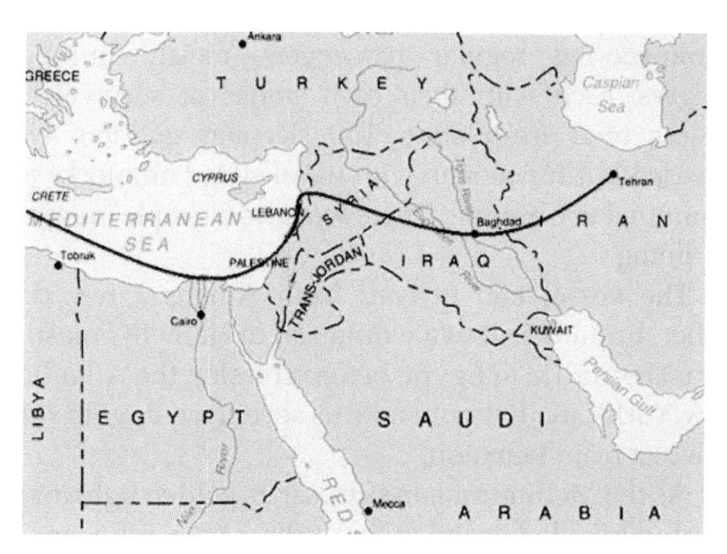

My travel route through Iraq and Syria to Beirut, Lebanon, on my way to America in July 1947

The following day, on the morning of my departure, Krista handed me a carefully wrapped package just before I stepped into the car that would carry me to the Iraqi border. She asked that I not open it until I was aboard the ship to America. Though I found her request curious, I agreed and embraced her before starting my long trip.

I traveled by bus through the rugged landscapes of Iraq and Syria, eventually reaching Lebanon. The next leg of the journey began at the Port of Beirut. Beirut was more than a city; it was a cultural hub, a hospitable oasis—some even called it the "Switzerland of the Middle East." I marveled at its vibrant streets, hearing French and Arabic, the scent of exotic foods, and the ever-present traditional Lebanese coffee. This cosmopolitan city was so different from Tehran and far more exciting. But it was only a temporary haven.

Several days later, we left Beirut en route to Haifa on board the *Marine Carp*. This retrofitted U.S. Naval vessel had participated in the Allied landing at Normandy. Now, it transported regular passengers—mostly European refugees, each with their own stories of survival and dreams of a fresh start. The sleeping quarters were crowded but functional, with naval-style hammocks and communal washrooms. There was also a simple mess area for dining.

The vessel had arrived from Athens a few days earlier. From Beirut, we would sail to Haifa in Palestine, then Alexandria in Egypt, before crossing the Atlantic to New York City. It would take us seventeen days to reach America from Lebanon.

As the Mediterranean sun cast its golden light across the ship's deck, I gazed at the endless blue, reflecting on the twists and turns of fate that had brought me here—bound for America, a world away.

Then, I remembered the gift Krista had given me upon my departure. Keeping my promise to her, I waited until I was on the ship to unwrap it. Inside, I found a beautifully bound volume of Goethe's poems.

Nestled within its pages was the very poem she had once recited to me, the one that had given her the courage to accept Haj Mirza Ali Khan's proposal. But tucked inside, I also found an envelope. As the ship pulled away from the dock and the sea stretched before me, I opened the letter and began reading.

The Harmless Necessary Cat

Passenger ticket for travel on the *Marine Carp* from Beirut to New York - July 1947

My dearest Sohrab, there were things I could not reveal to you in Tehran, dangerous secrets and burdens too heavy for that turbulent time. However, as you move towards new horizons, I don't want you to leave with unanswered questions between us.

The night before I agreed to marry Haj Mirza Ali Khan, a discovery in the study altered everything. I found a hidden letter from Franz addressed to Arash. He wrote of a clandestine network within Germany, the Kreisau Circle, rebels determined to overthrow the Nazi regime.

'I have left my homeland,' Franz had confessed, *'not to abandon it, but to save it from the tyrants that suffocate it.'*

Arash, whose heart had never truly left Germany, was captivated. Franz detailed a desperate need for resources to be funneled through specific channels to aid their resistance. Arash had agreed he could help and disguised these efforts as routine business transactions, utilizing Abbas's transport company for operations. Franz asked Arash to tell no one in his letter and to burn it after reading it.

Arash, burdened by the weight of his choice, told no one, not even me, and accepted this isolation as a necessary shield to protect us. Unfortunately, he believed in Franz's noble façade. 'Every shipment you've orchestrated has been crucial,' Franz wrote in his letter. 'We are turning the tide, saving lives.'

Unbeknownst to Arash, there was no resistance; he was a cog in Franz's grand deception. This is why the Soviets suspected Arash of espionage in favor of Germany. They observed his dealings with Franz but were oblivious to the fact that Arash believed he was undermining the Nazis, not aiding them.

A grim realization struck me as I stood in the study reading Franz's letter that night. If the Russians considered Arash a German spy, as Haj Mirza Ali Khan's cousin had warned, we would lose everything. Even the two of us could have been detained as co-conspirators and our property confiscated.

But Haj Mirza Ali Khan's proposal offered a shield of protection. His influence would ensure we remained safe in his household. So, despite not wanting to, I accepted his offer. I knew you disagreed with my decision and probably thought I was betraying your brother's memory while still in mourning for him. But I did this to protect us from what Arash had unknowingly done and to preserve his legacy from the stain of espionage.

Take my gift of Goethe's poems as a reminder that beauty can be found even in darkness, like what I have discovered with

Omid. He is the radiant light born from the shadows of our past, a testament to life's mysterious ways.

When I thought the door to motherhood was forever closed to me, another opened, and through it came Omid, a cherished miracle I never anticipated. He is proof that even when all seems lost, there is always a possibility for new beginnings, for joy to emerge amidst sorrow. I have now found that joy.

I hope Goethe's words inspire you in the new world you're about to enter, guiding you to find beauty even in the darkest times.

With all my love, Krista.

Krista's words sliced through me as the cold grasp of the truth sank in. I regretted judging Krista for her decision to marry Haj Mirza Ali Khan. At the time, blinded by grief, I failed to see the true reason for her silent sacrifice. She had desperately sought to protect us from an overwhelming peril, forcing herself to tread a path she loathed for our sake.

As I stood at the ship's rail, lost in thought, the murmur of conversations caught my attention. The familiar melodies of the Polish language, which had come to mean so much to me through Gabriela, drew me towards the gathering of passengers. The sound warmed my still tender heart. Among the travelers was Jakub, a Jewish Pole, freed from the horrors of Nazi-occupied Europe. I introduced myself to him, and he asked where I was from.

When I said, "From Iran," he didn't understand and asked again, "From where?" with a hand to his ear.

I answered, "From Persia."

He said, "Oh yes, I have read about Persia in our holy book."

"There's another from your country," he added, "a Persian who fled Paris."

I got excited. "Really? How can I find him?"

"Look for him in the mess hall at six," Jakub said, referring to the evening meal. "That's his assigned shift."

We shared stories. I spoke of the Polish refugees I encountered in Tehran and perhaps dwelled too long on Gabriela, but I couldn't help it. When I asked him why he was on the ship, Jakub spoke of his ordeal as a refugee and told me about the *Judenjagd*, the Nazi-coordinated hunt for Jews, often aided by Polish informers.

Photo courtesy Liberty Picture Co.
MARINE CARP

His voice cracked with raw emotion as he spat, "It wasn't just the Germans. Some Poles..." his voice trailed off, "they suddenly looked at us differently, treated us like strangers.

"I believed Poland was my home, but then the Germans came. They rounded us up like cattle. I saw them forcing some men to jump from buildings, shooting them as they fell. I watched through a hole in the barn where I hid. It was terrifying seeing they were coming for you."

I asked quietly, "What about your neighbors, Jakub? Didn't any of the people you worked with, those who knew you, try to help?"

Jakub's hands tightened around the table's edge, his knuckles white. He shook his head slowly, lips pressed together as if searching for the right words.

"No," he finally said, his voice low.

"Not one. I thought for sure someone would. That someone would step forward, say something, do something. But all stayed silent."

His fingers drummed on the surface, a nervous rhythm breaking the stillness. "And strangely, I can't even blame them."

Jakub paused, rubbing the back of his neck.

"Their silence wasn't out of hate but out of fear. Fear of being the next target, of losing everything. That kind of fear—it makes you forget what's right. It makes you stand by when you know you shouldn't. It was easier for them to pretend nothing was happening. People can always find reasons to stay silent."

Jakub continued telling me the story of his grueling escape and his dream of reaching Palestine, far away from the horrors of Europe.

"And then they brought me to that 'forsaken place,'" he added.

I interrupted to ask him where that place was in Germany.

He gave me a surprised look, shook his head, and said, "No, not the German camp - that was before. The place I'm talking about is a British internment camp."

I was confused. Jakub began to unravel his story in more detail. Born in Krakow, Jakub's family had been shattered by the Holocaust's machinery of death. He'd defied capture by smuggling himself into the ghetto, believing it would be safer even though it was overcrowded and the conditions were abysmal. But eventually, the Nazis liquidated the ghetto, and those fit for labor, like Jakub, were sent to Bergen-Belsen, a forced labor camp.

Across from me sat a man whose face mirrored the turmoil of his past. His fingers absentmindedly scratched at his forearm as he recounted the harrowing tales of his imprisonment, drawing my attention to a series of faded numbers inked on his forearm.

I had never seen anything like it and innocently asked him, "Jakub, I'm curious; what's the story behind the numbers on your arm?"

He paused, with his gaze shifting to the markings. He seemed to travel back in time, reliving whatever those numbers represented.

He then looked up, "These numbers," he started, his voice thick with grief, "are the only identity I have had for a long time. In Bergen-Belsen, the Germans took everything from us—our names, our possessions, our very identities. This number became my new name, a constant memento of the hell I lived through."

Jakub then rolled up his sleeve, revealing the full extent of the numbering.

"They did this to us upon arrival at the camp, branding us as their property. Each number was a life they tried to erase, a story they wanted to end. But I survived."

Jakub's weathered face contorted. A flicker of defiance sparked in his eyes, momentarily battling with the despair that clouded them.

"This number," Jakub declared, a tremor running through his hand as he pointed to the ink. "It's a German scar, a brand they burned onto my flesh, but it's also my badge of survival, a tribute to the strength I never knew I had."

It was a quiet assertion of his spirit's victory over the forces that sought to destroy him.

I asked him, "So why did you say you were in a British internment camp?"

Instead of answering me, Jakub fell silent, his shoulders slumping slightly as he took a deep breath and said nothing. I wondered if I had asked something I shouldn't have. But after a moment, he raised his head and continued, his voice steadier.

"When the war ended, and our camp was liberated, we were souls adrift, refugees dreaming of a sanctuary. So we boarded a fragile, rickety ship so overcrowded you could barely move. We were headed for British-run Palestine. But instead of Palestine, we ended up in an internment camp in Cyprus."

"Cyprus?" I asked with surprise.

Jakub, his voice trembling with the irony of his savior-turned-captor, said, "Yes, in Cyprus, the English soldiers — whom I would have kissed the feet of for liberating me in Germany — lept into our little boat with batons."

I asked, "Why did they do that?"

"The British were limiting Jewish immigration to Palestine, so they tried to stop boats ferrying war refugees," he explained, unearthing buried memories.

He told me that in the internment camp in Cyprus, the British herded them behind barbed wire, a cruel symbol of the nightmare they had fled. Jakub spoke of the austere and isolated camp where he was detained along with thousands of other Jews. People who survived the Holocaust or fled the post-war devastation in Europe, only to find themselves caught in the throes of another confinement.

"After all that, we were back behind barbed wire again," Jakub sighed. "In the camp, we lived in limbo, clinging to the dream of reaching Palestine."

And with great excitement, Jakub said he still couldn't believe he would be there soon. He was overjoyed to finally see the land his parents and grandparents had longed for but never had the opportunity to visit. This fulfilled a dream his ancestors had only dared to whisper back in Europe.

As invaders and occupiers in Iran, the British hadn't been kind to Iranians either. But putting regular civilians behind barbed wire fences, trapping them in cramped living quarters—especially those who had already endured such mistreatment by the Nazis—was extremely troubling.

I think Jakub didn't want me to equate what the Germans had done in Bergen-Belsen with what the British had done to him in Cyprus, so he softened his anger at his most recent captors, attempting to explain.

"In the camp, the English didn't starve us, and they weren't killing us like the Germans," he told me. "But it was so traumatic that the very same people who had liberated me just a short time ago were now incarcerating me."

We sat in silence for a moment, acknowledging the weight of his painful memories as the heaviness of Jakub's story hung between us. As much as I wanted to understand everything he had been through, the details of his suffering were becoming too much. I needed to find a way to step back, to take a break from the intensity of it all.

As dinner time approached, I remembered Jakub's earlier mention that the man from Iran could be found in the mess hall. Saying I wanted to meet him seemed like the respectful way out.

"Maybe now would be a good time for me to meet the Persian you mentioned," I said quietly, hoping Jakub would agree.

The Harmless Necessary Cat

He looked at me and nodded, realizing from my expression that I was overwhelmed. "Yes, yes, now is the time," he said softly.

I excused myself, went to the mess hall, asked around, and finally found the Persian. He was a slender man in his late thirties, sitting alongside a few other men speaking in French. I approached him and introduced myself in Persian.

"A Polish man I met said you are an Iranian who left Paris. I'm also from Iran and am traveling to New York to study."

His face brightened the moment he heard his mother tongue.

"Salam, my name is Eshagh (Isaac). It's so rare to hear Persian out here," he said warmly. "It's been years since I left Iran."

We exchanged stories about our homeland. Isaac wanted to know about my life in Tehran and recent events there. He told me he left his hometown of Hamadan years earlier to study in France.

After some small talk, I asked, "How is it that you're on this ship?"

He said, "When the Germans occupied France and Paris fell, the Gestapo made it mandatory for Jews to register with the police. At first, I didn't know if that applied to me, being a Persian Jew, but I didn't want to take any chances."

"So what did you do?" I asked.

Isaac took a deep breath. "I decided to go to the Iranian embassy. I thought they could tell me what to do. When I arrived at the front desk, a woman asked to look at my papers. When she saw them, she asked me if I was Jewish."

He hesitated, then added, "I told her the truth—yes, I was. A young man who must have overheard our conversation approached me. He called me into his office. I didn't know what to expect. He was calm and told me not to register with the police. He promised he would help me."

"What kind of help?" I asked.

"He told me to come back in a few days and that he would prepare some documents for me. He had a small darkroom in his office where he took my photo for a new passport. He told me it was too dangerous to go to a commercial studio—they might report me. So he did everything himself."

Isaac continued, "I later discovered he wasn't just a diplomat. He was also a lawyer, a brilliant one, using his legal knowledge to argue that we, Persian Jews, were Aryans under the Nazi racial laws and that the decrees didn't apply to us.

"But this honorable man wasn't just arguing to buy us time. He was forging documents—to get us out of France. He even helped some non-Iranian Jews. Many French Jews had already been taken from Paris to places like Auschwitz. Most never returned. I was one of the fortunate ones; I owe him my life."

I felt proud of a fellow Iranian's ingenuity and asked the man's name. Isaac replied, "His name is Sardari."

Isaac's story of Sardari made me think of Haidar, another Iranian who had risked his safety to help others during the war. Though they were separated by background and circumstance, both men shared an unshakable commitment to doing what was right, even in the face of unimaginable danger. Despite being thousands of miles apart, these brave souls found opportunities for heroism amid the chaos and destruction.

The Harmless Necessary Cat

Abdol Hossein Sardari, Consul General of Iran in Paris During World War II.

The war may have been all-encompassing, threatening to crush everything in its path, but it also revealed a quieter, more personal kind of courage. Haidar, Sardari, and men like them refused to let fear dictate their actions. Instead, they became beacons of hope to those who had lost everything. Their acts of defiance were a reminder that humanity's capacity for compassion and bravery endures even in its darkest hours.

Hearing these survivors' stories made me see how wrong I was when I told Karl, "The enemy of my enemy is my friend." I came to understand that Germany was no exception and no friend—it, too, was an occupier, akin to the Russians and British in Iran.

In my conversation with Karl about the war, I had rashly expressed a desire that the Germans prevail so the British and Russians would finally be driven out of Iran. Karl had gently warned me then, "You may unknowingly be praying for a different occupier if Germany wins."

I couldn't grasp the truth in what he expressed at the time, consumed by fury over Iran's subjugation. Only later did I realize that swapping one tyrant for another was no actual change at all but the continuation of a cycle of ongoing oppression.

Isaac told me he was going to Palestine with a group of French Jews who had escaped Nazi persecution in France. I recalled the only other Iranian Jew I had met, Mr. Kahan, my father's friend from the bazaar, who seemed content living in Iran.

So I asked Isaac, "Why didn't you return to Iran? Don't you have family in Hamadan?"

He drew a heavy sigh, "Iran, though the land of my ancestors, no longer feels like home. It is my birthplace, but it seems like a distant memory. What I saw in France haunts me. I'm fearful that what took place in France could also happen in Iran. I'll send for my family once I'm settled in Palestine."

He added, "The next time, such an angel might not be looking out for us. I would have never thought it could happen in Paris, of all places, but it did."

Isaac's statement about not wanting to return to Iran was delivered with a slight forward lean as if he were reaching out, seeking a silent communion of empathy. But his expression changed when he spoke of Palestine, where he aimed to anchor his future.

"It's the land where I hope to find peace and rebuild my life," he said. "I know it won't be easy, but I must believe in a better tomorrow," as he navigated the delicate balance between letting go of one homeland and cautiously embracing the possibility of a new beginning.

It seemed as though everyone I met had a frightening story. Tales of survival, loss, and unimaginable suffering poured out endlessly, as if each person's ordeal was competing to surpass the next. And these were the fortunate ones—those who had somehow endured and now clung to the hope of a better future. Their voices, though heavy with grief, were at least heard.

But for every survivor, there were countless others whose stories would never be told, silenced by death before they could even dream of escape. Their experiences, perhaps far more horrifying, remained buried with them—lost to the ravages of war. A stark reminder that the weight of suffering stretched far beyond the voices that could still speak.

Haifa, Palestine, 1947

On the *Marine Carp*, we carried more than just the invisible thread of shared suffering that connected us. For a fleeting moment, each of us, a refugee from something, found ourselves bound together in that transient world between worlds.

Understandably, excitement spread among those preparing to disembark in Palestine. When we reached the port of Haifa, I also felt a surge of emotion when I saw the place I had heard so much about during the journey.

I recalled Gabriela's quote: "...*Fools stand on their island of opportunities and look toward another land...*" But none of us on the ship felt like fools for chasing what we sought. As Thoreau suggested, we had *'launched ourselves on the waves'* and felt empowered. Within each of us was something intangible, yet fiercely our own—a dream of new beginnings and hope reborn on distant shores.

Epilogue

"The opposite of love is not hate, it's indifference."
Elie Wiesel

In May 1948, a few months after I arrived in New York, I heard the heartbreaking news that a war had erupted in Palestine. What the newly established Jewish state of Israel would call the "War of Independence," the existing Palestinian Arab population—who had lived there for generations—would call the "*Nakba*," or "the Catastrophe."

As a result of this war, more than 700,000 Palestinian Arabs—about half of the prewar Arab population of Palestine—were forced to flee or were expelled by militias and the Israeli army, with over 500 Arab villages destroyed in the conflict.

As the new state was carved out amidst the bloodshed and the steady influx of immigrants, I couldn't help but recall those who had once been refugees themselves. The Jewish survivors who disembarked in Haifa, escaping the ashes of Europe, were seeking refuge from the torment they had endured. But in their desperate quest for a place to call home, had they unknowingly become participants in creating another people's nightmare?

I remembered the faces aboard the ship—etched with the scars of Europe's war. I thought back to Jakub, who spoke fervently of building a new life, laying the foundations for a future where he could thrive without fear. But did he hear the cries of those whose lives were uprooted to make way for his dreams? And what of Isaac? Did he wish he had returned to Iran instead?

What kind of world is it where ceaseless wars and revolutions create a devastating cycle of displacement, forcing innocent people to leave their homes, driven by the dread of persecution and violence? Each new conflict spawns a fresh wave of exiles, often unsettling those who were displaced before. It is a tragic, endless carousel of human misery.

The aftermath of World War II affected countless lives around the world. Its impact was profound and far-reaching, exposing the deep despair that war leaves in its wake.

Still, even amid such devastation, the fragile promise of a new day persists. With that promise comes the responsibility to recognize our shared humanity, especially in times of conflict and suffering.

As I reflected on the hardships I had witnessed and the stories I had gathered along my journey through the war, the timeless words of the Persian poet Sa'adi echoed in my heart, reminding me of an enduring truth:

> *"All human beings are members of one frame,*
> *Since all, at first, from the same essence came.*
> *When time afflicts a limb with pain,*
> *The other limbs cannot at rest remain.*
> *If thou feel not for other's misery,*
> *A human being is no name for thee."*[1]

---

[1] The poem *"Bani Adam"* (Sons of Adam) from *"Gulistan"* (The Rose Garden) is the work of the poet Sa'adi of Shiraz (1210-1292). It adorns the entrance of the United Nations alongside a carpet gifted by the people of Iran.

Printed in Great Britain
by Amazon